DONALD RUSSELL
ROBERTSON

WORD PUBLISHING
Dallas · London · Sydney · Singapore

DEAR YOU

Unless otherwise indicated, all Scripture quotations are from the Revised Standard Version of the Bible, copyrighted 1946, 1952, © 1971, 1973 by the Division of Christian Education of the National Council of the Churches of Christ in the U.S.A. and are used by permission. Those marked KJV are from the authorized King James Version. Those marked NIV are from the New International Version of the Bible, published by the Zondervan Corporation, copyright © by the New York Bible Society International. Used by permission. Those marked TLB are from the Living Bible, copyright 1971 by Tyndale House Publishers, Wheaton, IL. Used by permission.

Library of Congress Cataloging in Publication Data

Robertson, Donald Russell, 1911–1987.
    Dear you / Donald Russell Robertson.
        p.   cm.
    ISBN 0–8499–0677–6
    1. Meditations. I. Title.
    BV4832.2R585 1989
    242—dc19   88–35964
                                                   CIP

Printed in the United States of America

9801239 MP 987654321

CONTENTS

AUTHOR'S INTRODUCTION

Dear You,

In 1975, I sat before my typewriter staring at a blank sheet of paper, wondering what in the world I would write that would draw people to church. I had run out of "rousements," pleas, and promotions. Everything I thought to say sounded so familiar and dull.

Then a thought struck me. Instead of telling the people that they would get an inspiration next Sunday, why not try to send them an inspiration right now? I wrote my first "Dear You" letter.

I have been humbled by the response. The members of the Church of the Marina read them; they shared them; they requested that relatives and friends be put on the mailing list. Some even began putting the letters on file for later reference. Since Marina del Rey is a mobile community, many of our members moved away each year. When they did, they insisted that we send the "Dear You" letter to their new addresses. My dedicated associate minister, Bill Douglas, also added the names of many ministers to our mailing list. Each week, he sends out the letter to people from Florida to Alaska.

We began to get letters of appreciation from various parts of the country. Many of these urged me to put the "Dear You" letters together in book form.

So, I called on my eldest son, Don, a professor of Sociology, to do the job of sorting and selecting the letters, organizing and editing them, and preparing the manuscript for publication. It has been a joy for me, as a dad, to see him dedicating his training and skill to this task.

Now, here they are, one hundred selected "Dear You" letters.

I hope that you will laugh with me, cry with me, and pray with me as you read them.

A traveler on the Way,
Donald R. Robertson

NOTE:

My father, Dr. Donald Russell Robertson, died suddenly on April 20, 1987, at the age of seventy-five. Earlier the same day, he delivered this manuscript to the typist. I found the preceding statement—clearly intended to be his introduction to the book—lying on his desk, evidently written during the final hours of his life.

Donald Robertson, Jr.

THE WALKING STEEPLE
A Tribute to the Memory of
DR. DONALD RUSSELL ROBERTSON
1912–1987

When the old man walked by, they hardly noticed
    That morning on the Venice Beach.
But he saw them with his practiced eye
    Seeking those he wanted to reach.

As the years passed by, he came on his morning round
    With a joke for Cathy, the waitress
And a verse for Ben, the coffee-hound;
    Relieving the tension, lessening the stress.

He changed them from strangers into old friends;
    Those he loved had become Jesus' own people,
Being brought together into harmonious blends,
    Because this man to them was God's Walking Steeple.

One by one they came to the Marina's little church
    To get a pat on the back for the one gone off track.
And found the rainbow, the end of their search.
    The Rev's talks were love upon love, and fact upon fact.

He preached with his hands, his heart, and his feet;
    He loved them with his friendly Scottish smile.
He loved eight miles of them, his God-assigned beat.
    He brought his own revolution, Rev Robertson style.

He had his own frailties, he never covered nor lied.
    He knew man's weakness and God's loving strength.
He may not have touched them all, but God knows he tried;
    Seventy-five years of ministry's length.

The day after Easter, the year of Eighty-Seven,
    In the sixth mile of his journey down Encouragement's Trail,
God's little Scotsman was called home to heaven.
    Little is much; God's Word never fails.

Oh, there's a song in the Marina's morning wind
    That calls from the chorus of the hurts of the street:
"Who'll take the Lord's stories to Cathy and Ben?
    And give God's Good News; and take the Rev's beat?"

Jess C. Moody

ENJOY THE TRIP

Last summer, along with my two sons, Don and Tim, I sailed my old twenty-four-foot boat, *The Rev*, a round-trip from Marina del Rey to Catalina Island, a total distance of 102 miles.

I didn't enjoy it.

Why not? Fear!

There was no peace in my heart. I was afraid to take the trip and I was afraid while I was taking it. I was afraid the little outboard motor might fail. I was afraid the radio might not function. I was afraid the compass might be wrong. I was afraid we might run into a gale with howling winds and huge waves. What was a seventy-four-year-old man doing out in this wide ocean anyway? What if I had a heart attack?

Actually, the motor ran smoothly. The radio worked perfectly. The breeze filled the sails in fine style. The boat was steady and seaworthy. But I still had no peace in my heart. I was not really enjoying the trip.

When we arrived at Catalina, I was tired, limp, and nervous. I could not enjoy the arrival because I was already worried about the return trip. I fretted the whole time I was on that beautiful little island.

Three days after our arrival, at 9:00 A.M., we started for home. I was at the tiller, keeping my eye on the compass to keep it at 355 degrees, and anxiously looking at the distant horizon toward the mainland and home. But not my two sons. They were sitting in the cabin.

Playing chess. Eating everything in sight.

The sea was as smooth as glass. The little outboard ran smoothly and steadily. There was no wind. After about three hours, we saw the mainland. My two sons yelled, "Yippee!" I breathed a huge sigh of relief.

At this point, Tim took over the tiller, a brisk wind came up, our sails filled, and we sailed into Marina del Rey and put

the old boat back into her familiar slip. We all hugged each other. Tim yelled, "Dad, we made it!"

Then a thought struck me. Suddenly I felt very guilty. Here I am, a minister who preaches about the peace that comes from trust in God, and never once during the whole trip had I even had one thought about God. No wonder I had no peace in my heart. No wonder I didn't enjoy the trip.

A Bible verse filled my mind and heart, "Thou wilt keep him in perfect peace, whose mind is stayed on thee, because he trusteth in thee" (Isaiah 26:3 KJV).

We are all on a trip. Sometimes we have smooth seas. Sometimes we face heavy seas and contrary winds. But we can have peace of heart if we have our minds stayed on Him.

Have faith and enjoy the trip!

A TIME TO WEEP . . . A TIME TO LAUGH

I have learned the hard way how true the Bible is when it says, "There is . . . a time to weep, and a time to laugh" (Ecclesiastes 3:1, 4).

What a tragedy it is when we are laughing while someone else is weeping. It happens all too often.

I remember an experience I had when I was a professor of psychology at Woodbury University in Los Angeles. I still cringe in shame when I think of it.

It was a very large class. I was the type of professor who would not tolerate talking in class or failure to attend regularly.

At the close of the first week of a new semester, as I was calling the names on the class roster, I noticed that Mr. Yamamoto had been absent for the first four days. Trying to assert my authority early in the semester, I jokingly remarked, "Mr. Yamamoto, I notice that you were absent the first four days of this class. What goes on here? Do you think this is a correspondence course?"

The student arose and quietly replied, "Dr. Robertson, my mother died in Chicago, and I had to fly home for the funeral. I just got back last night." Then he sat down.

Every student in the room hated me.

I hated myself.

I stood at the lectern feeling helpless, sick, and ashamed.

Finally, after a long and deafening silence, and in a somewhat tremulous voice, I said, "Mr. Yamamoto, I want to apologize to you and to this class. I was very wrong to do what I just did. I want you to know that I sympathize with you right now. I lost my own mother, and I know how much it hurts. I am really sorry, and I hope you will forgive me for being so insensitive."

There was no use continuing. Everything I tried to say sounded unnecessary and hollow. I dismissed the class and personally expressed my sympathy to the student.

16

It's all too easy to be insensitive. To be laughing when someone else is weeping. The smiling face does not always tell the true story. Often behind the smiling face there is a weeping heart. Sometimes we try to be cute when we ought to be caring.

"There is a time to weep and a time to laugh."

It really hurts when you get them reversed.

Dear You

BE STILL

There is a pause that refreshes!

It is so easy to be busy, busy, busy. It seems to be the demand and expectation of the day for that "successful" person always to be running on a treadmill of unending events and responsibilities. But it is quite possible to be "busy unto death."

It is probably true that, in the words of the old saying, "The Devil finds mischief for idle hands to do," but it is also true that he can keep us so incessantly busy we never have time to tune into the presence of God.

Reflection and meditation are almost lost words in this generation. We're going too fast, most of the time, to be able to slow down long enough to experience real reflection and meditation. I asked a minister how much time he spent in prayer. "Pray?" he said, with a quick chuckle, "I don't have time to cross myself."

The whirlpool of activity which is constantly sucking our "quiet hours" away from us is the most pernicious Frankenstein ever put forth in the name of success. We need to stop and ask ourselves not where we are going, but Why? And also, Why so fast?

Under the continuous pressure of activity, the meditative aspect of the Christian faith becomes merely a phase in the historical past instead of a reality in the hysterical present. Meditation is a "lost art."

Many times it seems as if some Satanic Director of life's ongoing motion picture is shouting, "Action! Action! Action!" And all of us seem to be straining and scrambling to play leading roles in the drama. Or, as Shakespeare put it, we are all "strutting and fretting our moment upon the stage."

But what we actually need to do, is to retire to some quiet spot and take a long, prayerful look at the script.

Some years ago, I had to drive from downtown Los Angeles to Manhattan Beach for a counseling session. I was feeling tired and nervous about many personal concerns as I struggled through the late-afternoon, bumper-to-bumper traffic. At long last, I arrived at the beach. I had about an hour to spare before my seven o'clock session so I parked my car and walked across the white sand toward the sound of the breakers crashing on the surf. In the distance, the red sun was just dropping below the horizon. No one else was on the beach. The lights began popping on in the houses along the shoreline. I felt all alone.

But it was a nice feeling, a solid feeling. Alone? Not really. A verse from the Bible came into my mind: *"Be still,* and know that I am God"* (Psalm 46:10).

A LADY WHO CARED

I live on the second story of the Church of the Marina headquarters, across the street from a bird sanctuary pond covered by thick foliage. It is inhabited by ducks, chickens, geese, rabbits, and roosters which crow the local residents awake every morning.

From my observation post across the street, I watch Leigh Platte as she lovingly ministers to these birds and animals. Leigh, an attractive middle-aged blonde with blue eyes and a contagious smile, loves every one of these creatures. To her, they are all family. She mothers and cares for them daily. Every morning and every evening she is there, clothed in her green volunteer Animal Shelter jacket, arriving each time with huge boxes of food. Soon she is in the midst of the noisy, scurrying animals, giving out the vegetables and other food. Besides her caring ministry at the "duck pond," Leigh works a full-time job. But this is her first priority.

Now you will understand why Leigh Platte's heart was broken when she arrived one recent morning to find that some sadistic intruder had crawled over the high fence during the night and had then held some of the chickens under water till they drowned and gouged out the eyes of some of the other creatures. It tore her up. She was crushed.

There, by the water, in the shadows of the foliage, surrounded by her watching and waiting flock, Leigh sobbed out her anguish and sorrow.

But the birds and animals were waiting to be fed. So, brushing away her tears, and with a heavy heart, Leigh was soon busy unloading the food for her precious brood.

Determined that such a terrible thing would not happen again, she has formed a group called "The Volunteers and Friends of the Bird Sanctuary." She has circulated a personal letter to those who live nearby, asking them to help look out for her flock.

Every time I look down from my bedroom balcony and see her green jacket moving around near the pond, I have a feeling of great inspiration. Yes, and envy. A quiet prayer arises in my heart: "Lord, help me to love and care for people as this woman does for her flock."

Caring is the name of the game.

PROMISES, PROMISES

Did you ever realize how important promises are in our lives?

We make promises, significant promises, when we get married. We make promises of our time and effort to our employers. We make promises to pay our doctors, our dentists, our phone bills, our car and house payments, our credit card expenditures, our church pledges, and so on. What would we do without promises?

When I was about five years old, my dad promised to take my sister, Alma, my brother, Doug, and me, to a park near the Detroit River in Windsor, Ontario, Canada. Dad promised. That settled it.

Dad kept his promise to us, but it wasn't easy. Dad was too poor to have a car, but he did have a bicycle, and that would have to suffice. Bless his heart, he put us on the handlebars of the bike, one at a time. Then, puffing and blowing, he pedaled each of us to the park nearly two miles away. He barely had time to catch his breath before he had to begin the task of taking us all back home on the same teetering old bike.

But he did it. He kept a promise I still remember, with a warm and grateful heart, well over a half century later.

It also warms my heart to know that God has made promises, and He keeps His promises, too.

The apostle Peter, the converted fisherman, writes, "By which have been given unto us exceeding great and precious promises, that ye may be partakers of the divine nature" (2 Peter 1:4 KJV). *Partakers of the divine nature.*

Now, that *is* a promise.

The apostle John, who was faithful to the end, says, "If we confess our sins, he is faithful and just, and will forgive us our sins and cleanse us from all unrighteousness" (1 John 1:9). Forgiveness from *all* our sins.

Now, that *is* a promise.

God promises, "I will instruct thee and teach thee in the way which thou shalt go" (Psalm 32:8 KJV). Divine guidance, with God as our personal "lookout."

Now, that *is* a promise.

Jesus promises, "Come unto me, all ye that labor and are heavy laden, and I will give you rest" (Matthew 11:28). Rest from labor and burdens.

Now, that *is* a promise.

Jesus promises, "If ye abide in me, and my words abide in you, ye shall ask what ye will and it shall be done unto you" (John 15:7 KJV). Assurance of answered prayer.

Now, that *is* a promise.

And that is not the end. In fact, there is no end. Jesus promises, "I am the resurrection and the life; he that believeth in me, though he were dead, yet shall he live" (John 11:25 KJV). Death does not end it all. Eternal life is a fact.

Now, that *is* a promise.

A promise is only as good as the character of the one making the promise. All *these* precious promises come from the heart of a God who is like Jesus Christ.

He can be trusted. So, trust!

Don't Settle for Leftovers

Years ago I was playing golf in the midafternoon of a very hot, dry summer day. I was "dying of thirst," but I could find no drinking fountains or machines dispensing any kind of drinks. So I trudged along with my mouth getting drier all the time and my eyes constantly scanning for something to drink. What I really wanted was an ice-cold soft drink, but I would have gladly settled for a water-faucet or hose at that point.

Finally, I spotted a Coca-Cola® bottle in a soft drink box that had been filled with ice. I couldn't believe my good luck. Alongside the box were crates filled with empty Coke bottles. Two little boys stood nearby. I ignored the boys as I hurriedly pried the cap off the bottle of Coke. I drank the whole bottle down in one long guzzle. It seemed to me that the cola was a bit flat and somewhat on the warm side; also, I reflected that the cap seemed to have come off rather easily.

Just then, one of the little boys standing there said to me, "Mister, did you drink that bottle that was in the box there?"

"I sure did," I replied. "Why?"

The two boys looked at each other sheepishly. One of the boys was obviously trying to suppress a giggle. The other said in a guilty voice, "Well, Mister, what we did was to take all the empty bottles and pour what was left in them into that one bottle. Then we pushed a cap on the bottle and put it in that box with the ice."

I gulped. So did my stomach. I had just downed the contents of stale, leftover Coke from the bottles of at least fifty people. My vivid imagination went wild. I felt the immediate need for a package of Tums.

But no harm came of it. I survived.

There is a message here. So many times in life we settle for stale leftovers when God wants to give us the fresh, clean "water of life." Jesus says, "Whosoever drinketh the water that I shall give him shall never thirst again" (John 4:14 KJV).

We do not need to settle for worldly, stale, second-hand stuff. We can go to the Primary Source—to Jesus Christ Himself!

Don't ever settle for leftovers!

DEALING WITH DEATH

In 1972, I received a phone call that left me stunned. My Dad . . . dead! Though he'd lived for nearly nine full decades, I was unprepared for it. Engulfing loneliness struck. My dad seemed so durable. It seemed like he would always be there. Always just down the road. Always available.

Nothing is more realistic or more jarring than death.

But none of us likes to think much about death. We try in every way to push the thought of it out of our minds. Turn on the TV. How are the Rams doing? The Dodgers? Do things look better on the stock market? Oh, it's getting closer to vacation time. Say, hand me the Travel section of the newspaper. Come on, everyone, let's just "think positively."

On and on it goes. We have whole arsenals full of diversionary mental tactics to avoid the grim fact that death is inescapable. There is a deathly finality about it. There is one simple, solid fact that will not go away.

Death.

Death is certain.

Death can happen at any time . . . and does. The old *must* die. But the young *may.* We must constantly evaluate our lives in the shadow of death. Earthly arrangements and purely selfish plans must go. Death renders them meaningless.

If our lives are to have meaning, they must have meaning *now.* All that we are, or are becoming, must be realized this moment. Appropriate are the words of Jesus, spoken to the smug, rich farmer who was planning to build bigger and bigger barns: "Thou fool, this night thy soul shall be required of thee: then whose shall those things be?" (Luke 12:20 KJV).

You've heard it said, "Today is the first day of the rest of your life." True, but it could also be the *last* day of your life. So remember, "This is the day that the Lord hath made" (Psalm

118:24 KJV). It belongs to Him. So do we. We should be all His, all day.

What I am trying to say is that the reality and certainty of death should jar us to reality and the certainty of life—life in Christ. We never really face life until we face death. They are both wonderfully and terribly real.

Paul triumphantly looked death in the face and sang out, "For to me to live is Christ, and to die is gain" (Philippians 1:21). Living each moment in Christ takes the "sting" out of death.

Is death an immediate certainty? Yes. But so is Christ!

As Christians, we are on the living side of death because we are merged with Him who said, "I am the resurrection and the life: he that believeth in me, though he were dead, yet shall he live" (John 11:25 KJV).

Lord, in the shadow of death, we see the Light of life.

A Parable in a Pigeon

In a world of confusing road maps, "alternative lifestyles," manifold cultures, and contradictory "world views," it is often hard to know where to go and even harder to know how to get there. This is why the theme of God's guidance is so special to me. And why the evidences of God's "guidance-systems" within the natural world are so fascinating to me.

The pigeon gives us a marvelous example.

A number of years ago, the teenage son of a dear friend of mine told me, with great animation and obvious excitement, about his newly acquired homing pigeon. He said the bird had first made several short flights home from short distances away, all within the area of Long Beach, California.

Then came the big flight. With his eyes big and bright, the teenager told me how he, along with his family, had taken a trip about 600 miles away from their Long Beach home. He had taken the pigeon along in the car as they drove through territory that was totally unfamiliar to the pigeon.

The boy said, "Was it ever fun! I let the pigeon go and it flew right straight up in the air. And then, it took off straight for Long Beach. When we got home in a couple of days, there was that pigeon, sitting in the coop waiting for us. Wasn't that something?"

Yes, it was something. Something very profound. I happened to mention this incident to one of my college classes at the time, and, after class, one of the students came up to me and said, "I have owned homing pigeons for a number of years, and I have worked with them and studied them. It is actually even more amazing than what you described. A pigeon cannot fly very high, so when it comes to a high mountain, it flies around till it finds a canyon, and then it finds a new flight path and keeps on heading for home."

Having once had my own airplane, I must say that this

navigational feat is astonishing to me. How can the pigeon keep finding a path for home, no matter where home is, or how far away from home it starts out, or how many obstacles it must circumvent on the way?

How big is a pigeon's brain? It's big enough for God to build into it a sophisticated navigational system that invariably brings it back home. Talk about the possibilities of "miniaturization"! What an example!

I cannot help but believe that if God can make such a remarkable arrangement for the guidance of a pigeon, He must have made no less trustworthy arrangements for my guidance. I am worth more to Him than a pigeon. So are you.

In fact, He said so, and it is worth repeating because God promises each of us a *personalized* guidance system—

"I will guide *thee* with mine eye" (Psalm 32:8 KJV).

INCOMPLETENESS

I was once having a counseling session with a woman in my office when I noticed that she kept looking nervously at the wall in back of my desk. She was staring right past me, and I couldn't seem to get her full attention. Finally, she could sit still no longer. She got up, walked around the desk and straightened a picture hanging on the wall. Then she sat down and, with an obvious sigh of relief, said, "I just can't feel comfortable when I see a picture that is hanging crooked on the wall."

But, do you know what? The older I get, the more convinced I am that there will always be "pictures hanging crooked on the wall." There will always be a lot of things that are not straight. I will never be able to put everything "in order." And neither will you. Life *is* incomplete. If we are to have any contentment in life, we will have to learn to surrender to the reality of this incompleteness.

This thought crashed in on me when I was in the hospital for open-heart surgery. I have always been a confessed coward, and I fully expected that I'd be totally gripped by a sense of fear.

But, to my peaceful surprise, I was instead caught up in an overwhelming and engulfing sense of incompleteness. I thought, *Hey, I can't just "up and die" now. There is too much that is incomplete, too many things utterly unfinished. There are so many books I haven't read, so many parts of the world I haven't seen yet, so much good music I haven't listened to, so much yet to do and to see, so many problems yet to solve. And there is so much human history literally unfolding before my eyes. No, I just can't leave now. There is too much incompleteness.*

That's when it hit me! Incompleteness is an unshakable fact of life. Life will never be *completely* completed. There will always be those annoying crooked pictures on the wall. There will always be books to be read, trips to take, papers to file, lawns to be mowed, chores to be done, et cetera, et cetera. Life will always be an unfinished sentence. If I am ever to be a contented person, I must learn to live and die with the fact of incompleteness. Let the pictures hang crooked on the walls of life. I will be a contented person.

The apostle Paul says, "I have learned, in whatever state I am, to be content . . . . I can do all things in him who strengthens me" (Philippians 4:11, 13). Paul knew well the sense of the incompleteness of things. For him, there were always new churches to start, epistles to write, church problems to be sorted out, the needy to be cared for, new missions to be taken for the gospel. But Paul could be a contented man, in any and every situation, because he had strength from Christ.

Through complete surrender to the presence of Christ, we can learn to live in the presence of life's inescapable incompleteness.

STUMBLING IS PART OF THE GAME

On August 12, 1984, I stood on the balcony of my home and watched the Olympic Marathon runners puffing and pounding their way through Marina del Rey on their way to the finish line in the Memorial Coliseum some fifteen miles away. It was a grueling race. The sun was hot, the pavement was hard, and the hills were exhausting. To me, it looked like a victory just to stay alive!

I admired these dedicated long-distance runners as they struggled on and on, sweat pouring off their bodies and weariness showing in their faces. I cheered for them along with hundreds of thousands of others who lined the Marathon course that hot summer day.

There is a parallel to life here.

All of us are in the *race* of our life. And we all need to get all the encouragement we can. And, one thing is for sure, none of us gets a "trouble-free," easy-going race. For all of us, the pressure is always on.

And, stumbling is part of the game of life, as it is a part of sports competition. What happened in the women's Olympic 1500 meter race is a classic example. Mary Decker, the world-class runner from the U.S.A., and Zola Budd, born in South Africa but representing Great Britain, were the favorites to win. The world was watching the confrontation between these two stars of track and field.

On the second lap of the race, the two favorites were running nearly side by side at the front of the pack. Zola Budd, who was just barely leading the race, moved over to the inside lane and Mary Decker, who was struggling to forge into the lead, stepped on her heel. Zola wobbled for a second, but she managed to keep on going. Mary stumbled in pain. She fell hard to the turf inside the track. She was out of the race and

writing in agony. Zola Budd, shaken by the accident and in pain from the wound on her heel, finished a dismal seventh.

Yes, stumbling is part of the game. It even happened to the early Christians. Under the pressure of criticism and persecution and temptation, many became discouraged and began stumbling in their faith. The writer of the Book of Hebrews encourages them to keep on running the race: "Since we have such a huge crowd of men of faith watching us from the grandstands, let us strip off anything that slows us down or holds us back, and especially those sins that wrap themselves so tightly around our feet and trip us up; and let us run with patience the particular race that God has set before us" (Hebrews 12:1 TLB). "Keep your eyes on Jesus, our leader and instructor . . ." (Hebrews 12:2 TLB).

All of us are susceptible to discouragement, to depression (especially when we stumble), to being out-of-shape spiritually, and to being tempted to "just up and quit." Sometimes it seems like the race is too painful, too long, and too discouraging. But God has set the race before us. He put us in the race. And He told us to look to Jesus Christ, who ran right through the crucifixion to the resurrection.

In Him there is no way we can lose. So, keep running!

PERSON OR PROGRAM?

This morning I feel guilty and ashamed.

A couple of mornings ago, on Saturday, I hurried home from a meeting nearby so I could watch the National Open Golf Championship on television. I was especially excited and interested in this tournament because Bruce Devlin, a man in his forties who had rarely played golf for the past decade, was the surprising leader against all the best golfers in the world. I was pulling for the "old guy." I usually do, nowadays.

As I pulled up in front of my house, eager to get inside and find out if Devlin was still holding the tournament lead, I noticed a middle-aged, Latin-looking man slouched on the front lawn. His head was bent over, and he looked to be either drunk or spaced-out on drugs. Trying to avoid him, I quietly parked my car and entered the house. Happy that I had successfully escaped this man, I flipped on the TV. I was soon enthusiastically rooting for "the old guy" to win it all.

Then, abruptly, the doorbell chimes rang out. I waited. They rang again. As I pulled myself away from my comfortable chair and the television, I thought, *I hope it's not that guy I saw slumped on the lawn.* Very quietly, I peered through the peephole in the front door. There was the same man standing outside my door. That was exactly what I didn't want. This visitor was an utterly unwanted intruder.

So, trying to be silent as a church mouse (so to speak), I tiptoed back to the television. But the man seemingly wouldn't quit. The doorbell chimes rang again, and again, and then again.

I felt guilty, but I stayed put. I did not open the door. Finally, the chimes stopped ringing. I peeked out the door again. The man was gone.

So was my peace of mind.

Never before in my life had I refused to open my door to a person who came for help. I felt guilty and ashamed. Here was this apparently drunken man looking up at the large cross on our building through his bleary eyes, assuming that here he would find help. And I, the minister, had refused to open the door to him.

Oh, I tried to defend myself, at first, by thinking, *Well, the man was drunk, and if I had given him money he would just have gone down to the liquor store and bought some more booze.* But still, I felt miserable. I still do. I had closed the door of my house, and, worse, I had closed the door of my heart. The TV program had been more important to me than a needy person. I can still hear the doorbell clanging!

I learned again a painful lesson: persons are always more important than programs. In fact, I am surprised at myself, responding as I did. All my life I have tried to be responsive to people's needs. Often I have been "taken" by being "open" to people. But this time I failed.

There are people who come into all our lives who are saying in their own ways, "Help me." Let's open our hearts . . .

Or the bells will keep clanging!

EVERYBODY WANTS STROKES

I have a new resident in my home—a huge nineteen-pound cat called Boa. He arrived with Jim and Jan Negrucci when they moved here from the South and temporarily lived with me while locating a house for themselves.

They warned me that Boa was a recluse of the worst kind and notoriously unfriendly. I soon noticed how right they were. For days, Boa would disappear. The invisible cat. He was a master at hiding. After everyone was bedded down at night, he would sneak out and eat his food, and, fortunately, visit the litter box. The Negruccis assured me that he wasn't mad at me. He had always been this way.

Jim and Jan found a place to rent, but no pets were permitted. So I agreed to keep Boa. I was also determined that his days of ignoring me were over. Each day I would seek him out.

At first, he was not at all enthusiastic. In fact, he was downright resentful. When I would pick him up in my arms, he would hold his body rigid, all the while looking for a place to jump and land.

I would just keep on stroking him. Gradually I enticed him out of hiding with a piece of chicken here and bit of tuna there. Always stroking him. Sometimes he would lie on his back and let me stroke under his chin. His eyes would close. He seemed happy and relaxed.

Before long Boa became a delightful nuisance. He was everywhere. In the middle of the night, he would plop his nineteen pounds on my bed. To get my attention, he would zig-zag in front of my legs as I walked down the stairs.

When my associate, Bill Douglas, sat down to work in his office, there was Boa stretched out in the middle of his desk. Boa got what he wanted. Bill would stroke him, too. When we sat down around the long table for our Bible study, Boa would sprawl himself out in the middle of the table.

It worked. Everybody stroked him. Now, every time I go to the kitchen, he joins me, begging for snacks or strokes—or both.

What made the difference? Stroking. Boa wanted to be stroked. We all do. All of us sometimes feel inadequate. We all want to feel loved. We want to know that someone cares. We want to feel encouraged. We want to feel important.

The Bible tells us to encourage and lift up one another. How eternally encouraging it is to know that, "While we were yet sinners Christ died for us" (Romans 5:8).

The cross is a constant reminder that we are eternally important to God.

Make some person feel important today.

"Where's the Beef?"

Remember the TV ads that featured the phrase, "Where's the beef?"

The late Clara Peller, an over-eighty, gravel-voiced, four-foot, ten-inch grandmother from Chicago, barked these words in a Wendy's hamburger commercial that had politicians, comedians, and everyone else laughing at its needling message.

Clara, holding a large hamburger bun with a very small piece of meat in the middle, looked scornfully at it and growled, "Where's the beef?"

The message is clear. You have a big, showy hamburger, but it does not live up to its billing. It is actually a poor excuse for a hamburger. The size of the bun seems to promise much, but the burger delivers very little. It has very little substance, despite the appearance. There's very little beef.

You don't have to strain to apply this to the Christian life. Many people put on quite a promising religious "show" but produce very little Christian substance. I have seen all too many Christian people—including the one I see in the mirror—who can quote appropriate scriptures by the yard, who accurately pronounce the appropriate evangelical doctrines with appropriate unction, but who fail to show much appropriate Christian substance.

I have had to come to a tough conclusion: I am not just a bit overweight, I'm fat! My brother, Tom, with brotherly candor, recently said to me, "Don, I don't know what diet you're on, but whatever it is, it's not working." Oh, sure, I was well informed about calories, starches, and proteins, about vegetables and fruits and exercise, and all the other shibboleths. But my weight was a lot more convincing than my words. A fat person is simply a poor ambassador for slimness.

We've all heard it said, "What you do speaks so loud I can't hear what you say."

You can take it from there:

- A stingy person talking about generosity.
- A hot-tempered person talking about calmness and poise.
- An impatient person talking about patience.
- A prayerless person talking about the power of prayer.

When this happens, people will be inclined to ask—"Where's the beef?"

BREAKTHROUGH

Near the city of Edinburgh, Scotland, stands the majestic Firth of Forth Bridge. Completed in May, 1880, it has a center span of 1710 feet. It was then the longest cantilever bridge in the world. At that time, it was one of the engineering wonders of the world.

The day for the completion and dedication of the bridge arrived. For many long months, two separate work crews had been working toward each other from opposite sides of the bay. Now the time had come when the two huge steel structures would be connected in the middle of the bay. What a glorious day it was!

Everyone who could find a way to come was there for the great day. Countless boats bobbed on the water, people by the thousands lined the shores, dignitaries from various parts of the world came together to witness the joining together of the two sections of the bridge. Bagpipe bands filled the air with distinctively Scottish music. It was a proud moment for the people of the "wee" country of Scotland.

Then came the giant shock! The two sections of the bridge would not come together. Officials began to squirm in embarrassment and humiliation as the steel workers sweated futilely under the overcast sky. But there was still a gap that refused to be closed.

The bridge builders tried everything they could think of: tugboats tugged, cables strained, tractors pulled, cranes lifted. but the gap remained. They rechecked the blueprints. Everything seemed to be correct. So why the gap? Despair set in as they ran out of options. Their spirits were as low as the clouds hanging in the sky.

Suddenly something happened! The warm sun broke through the overcast. The warm rays beamed down on the cold metal of the bridge. As the officials watched, an apparent miracle took place before their eyes. The gap between the two sections of the bridge began to gradually close. Warmed by the sun, the two long sections of the bridge began to inch toward each other high above the bay. In a while, the two sections came flush together. Hurriedly, the work crews put in the bolts and the bridge was finally fastened together. An enormous cheer went up along with a great sigh of relief.

In all of our individual lives, there are tangled times when things just won't fit together. We sweat, struggle, and try everything humanly possible, but we still can't make things come together. The sky is overcast and our spirits droop. Feelings of futility, anguish, even panic, set in. Then the warmth of God's love breaks through the gloom and—miraculously—things begin to fit together. Behind the overcast skies . . .

He has been there all the time!

LET GO AND LET GOD

Security is the name of the game.

Especially is this true in our relationship to God. To try to hang on to God is very tiring and very precarious.

I saw a good illustration of this in 1943 when I was a seminary student and pastor in Mountain View, California. I was walking to church one Sunday morning with my frisky, three-year-old son, Don. He was holding my hand as we walked along together. Then, without warning, Don missed his step and went sprawling on the sidewalk.

He was not hurt, but to avoid this happening again I took a firm hold of his little wrist. Sure enough, his boundless energy caused him to stumble several more times before we got to the church. But now the outcome was altogether different. When he would stumble, I would hold firmly to his wrist, and he would swing back and forth till his feet were back on the ground. What a difference it made when the father was holding on to the son instead of the son holding on to the father.

Our heavenly Father is not only the Divine Seeker, he is also the Divine Keeper. We are the recipients of both the "Divine initiative" and the "Divine tenacity."

If my security is only as strong as my human faith and strength, then I am in real trouble. All of us are prone to sinfulness and stumbling. We all get tired trying to hang onto God, too pooped out to feel much security or peace. Our security is in God's grip, not in ours.

Jesus says, 'No man is able to pluck them out of my Father's hand" (John 10:29 KJV).

Paul says, "He is able to keep that which I have committed unto him . . ." (2 Timothy 1:12 KJV).

There is also the lovely affirmation: "Thou wilt keep him in perfect peace whose mind is stayed on thee" (Isaiah 26:3 KJV).

Our security is not man-centered but God-centered. Our security is in a Christlike God. He is the "peacekeeping force" in our lives.

Lord, help us to "let go and let God."

Dear You

THE BLACK BANTY ROOSTER

When I started out in the ministry, I was so obviously a minister it would shock you. Trying to imitate a minister I knew, I wore a black suit, tie, hat, and shoes. (I probably would have worn black shorts too if I could have found them.) I wanted everyone to know that I was, indeed, a minister, "a man of the cloth." I wanted to give everyone the impression that there was a holy man in their midst.

My "ministerial" garb did not impress Dr. Lumbar, a retired minister, one of my early teachers and counselors, and a man I greatly admired. One day, trying to keep his grin from breaking out into a laugh, he remarked, "You know, Don, as you were walking up to our house, I thought to myself, *Don looks like a black Banty Rooster.*"

I didn't share his amusement. Inwardly, I had a shuddering shock. I felt humiliated and disillusioned.

But I also found that I was somehow relieved. It's a strain to be "on stage" day after day. I vowed never to be a "black Banty Rooster" again. I determined to try to be real to myself, to God, and to others. I would try to be more spiritual than people think I am rather than less spiritual than they think I am. I have a growing hatred of all phony spirituality—in myself or in others. Phony spirituality invariably blocks us from the real thing, that is, a genuine and joyous relationship with God.

Jesus had scorching words for those who parade an insincere rather than a genuine spirituality: "When you pray, don't be like hypocrites who pretend piety by praying publicly on the street corners and in the synagogues where everyone can see them. Truly, that is all the reward they will ever get. But when you pray, go away by yourself, all alone, and shut the door behind you and pray to your Father secretly, and your Father, who knows your secrets, will reward you" (Matthew 6:5 TLB).

Spiritual reality is "an inside job." A phony faith keeps it on the outside. To have a real God, we have to be real persons. Take a tip from Popeye, who said, "I yam what I yam, and dat's what I yam."

Lord, make me real so that You will be real.

THE LEAVES OF AUTUMN

The grim faces of the doctors told the story. They had just completed an intensive study of the tests made on a young wife and mother of a five-year-old son. The woman's health had gotten progressively worse, and she was finally brought to the hospital for a complete check-up and definitive diagnosis.

The conclusion was sad and final. Cancer had already spread throughout her body. It was a terminal case. Six months to live!

The heavy-hearted husband bundled up his wife to drive her back to their small farm. It was a lovely spring day. Flowers were in full bloom, the birds were singing, the trees were covered with green leaves. Autumn was six months away.

The father, feeling that he should start preparing his little boy for the sad departure on the horizon, took the five-year-old aside and said to him, "Virgil, your mother is going to go away."

With the straightforward inquisitiveness of a child, Virgil asked, "When is she coming back?"

"She's not coming back," his father sadly replied.

Virgil paused for some time, then asked, "When is Mommy going away?"

Trying to soften the horrible news as much as possible, the father looked at the tree outside the window and said wistfully, "When the leaves start turning brown and falling off that tree, Mommy will have to go away."

The mother got weaker and weaker. The air began to chill. Autumn was near. The leaves on the tree outside the window began turning brown. Soon they would start to fall.

One day Virgil was missing. The father searched the pasture, the barn, and everywhere else, calling out his name. There was no response.

Finally the father spotted the son. There he was up in the

tree near the house with a handful of string. He was tying the brown leaves to the branches of the tree!

Oh, to capture the tenderness and innocence of a child! No wonder Jesus said, "Let the little children come to me . . . for to such belongs the kingdom of God" (Mark 10:14). It is also written that, "A little child shall lead them" (Isaiah 11:6).

When this story was told at a recent ministers' conference, you could feel a silent sob in the room. Now I have a reminder of my need for tenderness.

A falling leaf.

HIS PRESENCE MAKES THE DIFFERENCE

The Lord's Presence makes the difference.

There was a darling little girl staying at a summer hotel. She was of that age when small fingers are just beginning to find their way on the keyboard of a piano. Sitting one afternoon at the grand piano in the drawing room of the hotel, she was striking as many wrong notes as right ones, and she was not very sensitive to the anguish such discordant sounds can inflict on others.

A brilliant musician staying at the same hotel happened to enter the drawing room at that point. He quickly analyzed the situation, then he sat down beside her on the piano stool as she awkwardly thumped out her tune.

Without saying a word, he put his hands on the keyboard along with hers. He began to accompany her with exquisite improvisations. No matter what notes she struck, right or wrong, he would surround them with chords of surpassing beauty. The crowd in the drawing room soon became an audience. People watched and listened in amazement and admiration.

Then the performance was over. The brilliant musician took the little girl by the hand and faced the applauding audience. He introduced her as the one to whom they were indebted for the wonderful music. Her stumbling efforts had led to his magnificent accompaniment, but it was his part, of course, that had made the music memorable and inspirational.

It is the Lord's Presence in our lives that makes the difference. In my best moments I remember that. But too many times, the "self" and the things of "this world" crowd in and cloud the truth.

Jesus says, "For without me ye can do nothing" (John 15:5 KJV).

Paul says, "It is God which worketh in you both to will and to do of his good pleasure" (Philippians 2:13 KJV).

The "life more abundant," the "fruit of the Spirit"—these all come when, and only when, He plays on the keyboard of our hearts.

The Lord's Presence makes the difference.

"HOLD THE FORT"

Did you ever feel desperate wondering if help would ever come?

Think of how the hymn, "Hold the Fort," came to be written: Just before General Sherman of the Union Army began his famous "march to the sea" in 1864, and while his army lay encamped near Atlanta, the army of Confederate General Hood, in a carefully prepared movement, circled the right flank of Sherman's army, got behind him, and started the destruction of the railroad leading north, the main supply line for the Union army. Hood's soldiers were burning blockhouses and capturing small Union garrisons along the railway line.

Sherman's army was put rapidly in motion pursuing Hood to save the supplies and the larger posts, the principal one of which was located at Altoona Pass. General Corse of Illinois was stationed there with about 1500 men. A million and a half food rations were stored there and it was terribly important to the Union cause that the earthworks commanding the pass and protecting the supplies be held.

Six thousand men under the command of General French were detailed by Hood to take the position for the Confederate army. These troops completely surrounded the works, and the defenders were summoned by General French to surrender.

Union General Corse refused to surrender, so the fight was on. Slowly but surely the defenders were driven back from the pass into a small fort on the crest of a hill. The battle was bloody and bitter. The outnumbered Union soldiers fought bravely but suffered many casualties. Their plight was dim. It seemed hopeless to continue. They hung on, but their spirits were sagging.

Then something happened! A Union Officer caught sight of a signal flag far away across the valley, twenty miles distant, upon the top of Kenewaw Mountain.

The signal was answered, and soon a return message was waved back to them from mountain top to mountain top that sent their hopes skyward: "HOLD THE FORT: I AM COMING. W. T. SHERMAN."

Cheers filled the air. The Union soldiers gained new strength, and although they were under murderous fire for three solid hours, they held the fort until they were rescued by Sherman's army.

When P. P. Bliss, the famous hymn writer, heard this story from Major Whittle at a Sunday school meeting in Rockford, Illinois, in May, 1870, the great hymn, "Hold the Fort," was born in his mind. Listen to these words:

> Ho, my comrades, see the signal
>   Waving in the sky;
> Reinforcements now appearing,
>   Victory is nigh.
> Hold the fort for I am coming,
>   Jesus signals still;
> Wave the answer back to heaven,
>   By Thy Grace we will.

All of us have sometimes been battered and ready to give up. There have been moments when it seemed worthless to go on. That is when we need to look up and see God's signal flag of hope, and to hear His words: "When these things begin to take place, stand up and lift up your heads, because your redemption is drawing near" (Luke 21:28 NIV).

Greyfriar's Bobby

In Edinburgh, Scotland, there is a monument that was erected in honor of a faithful dog. It is a red granite fountain that provides drinking water for both people and dogs who pass by. On the top of the monument there is a life-sized model of a dog who is known throughout Scotland as "Greyfriar's Bobby."

In the mid-1850s, John Gray found a stray terrier wandering around the streets of Edinburgh. Gray took the dog in and gave him the name, "Bobby." Master and pet became inseparable until John died in 1858. Then Bobby became a stray dog again. For several days after John's death and burial, Bobby would dart back to the restaurant where his master had brought him daily at lunchtime. The restaurant owner tried to feed Bobby, but he would always run away. The owner began to wonder where the dog rushed off to so quickly, and so he finally followed Bobby. To his amazement, he found Bobby standing guard over John Gray's grave.

When the word spread about how Bobby spent his days in a constant vigil beside his master's grave in Greyfriar's Cemetery in Edinburgh, the faithful terrier became known as "Greyfriar's Bobby." People came from all over Scotland to see this famous dog and bring him food to eat.

For fourteen long years, until his own death, Bobby remained faithful beside John Gray's grave. Weather made no difference at all. There were drenching rains, howling winds off the Firth of Forth and the North Sea; there were punishing hailstorms and heavy snow. But Bobby never left his post. He was always there.

On the monument built in his honor, there is this inscription: "In tribute to the affectionate fidelity of Greyfriar's Bobby. In 1858 this faithful dog followed the remains of his master to Greyfriar's Cemetery and lingered near the spot until his death."

Faithfulness, like gold, is wherever you find it.

Faithfulness and love are tied together.

It is wonderful to know that when we are unfaithful to God, He is still faithful to us. Our security is not based upon our faithfulness, but His. "If we are faithless, he remains faithful—for he cannot deny himself" (2 Timothy 2:13).

We are not called to be successful, but to be faithful. Striving for "success" can be, and often is, an "ego trip." But faithfulness is a product of love. That is why we should have our hearts always tuned to hear the words of our Lord—

"Well done, thou good and faithful servant" (Matthew 25:21 KJV).

"THE ART OF PREACHING"

One of the paradoxical axioms of the Christian faith is that victory comes through surrender. That the way to be a winner is to be a loser. That the more one demands his own way, the more he loses *the* way. That self-assertion brings feelings of God's desertion. That when we think we are most strong, we are most weak. That when we are most childlike, we are most Godlike.

Jesus couldn't be more specific about this: "He that loseth his life for my sake shall find it" (Matthew 10:39 KJV). The apostle Paul is no less specific: "What things were gain to me, those I counted loss for Christ" (Philippians 3:7 KJV). Paul rejoices in the good news of the *freedom* we have through Jesus Christ, but he also revels in the fact that he is a *bondslave* of Christ.

In a world that constantly says "push yourself," it is hard to believe in "surrender" of self. The idea of finding ourselves by "losing" ourselves goes against the grain. It is hard to swallow. It doesn't go down easily. And the self doesn't die easily—even in preachers.

In 1944, I traveled to Green Lake, Wisconsin, for a ministers' conference. Riding in the bus which took us from the railroad station to the conference grounds, I happened to be seated alongside an older man with rumpled clothes, a wrinkled felt hat, and a battered briefcase. He was a nice, affable, sort of quiet old guy. His unimpressive appearance gave me the idea that he was probably pastor of some small country church.

Fresh out of seminary, I was full of new-found knowledge and abundant self-confidence. I was dressed in my best suit for maximum impact upon my fellow ministers.

Trying to be helpful to this old country preacher, I spent the whole trip sharing my insight into the Scriptures and my varied preaching techniques. That sweet old gentleman was so humble, so attentive, so kind and appreciative, that I talked steadily and with great animation till we arrived at Green Lake. I got off the bus feeling quite smug and satisfied—and helpful.

That night, at the opening meeting, the principal speaker of the conference stood up, following a glowing introduction, to speak on "The Art of Preaching."

He was the same old man I had lectured on the bus!

HUMPHREY THE HUMPBACK WHALE

A humpback whale discovered that a wrong turn can be a miserable and dangerous experience.

Remember Humphrey? He became the most famous humpback whale in history not so long ago. At forty tons, Humphrey was leisurely cruising and spouting his way southward to spend the winter months in the warm waters of the Pacific Ocean near the Hawaiian Islands. But he made an astonishing wrong turn. Instead of continuing southwest, he made an unprecedented left turn into the San Francisco Bay, swimming under the huge and threatening Golden Gate Bridge. He ended up seventy miles inland on the muddy shallows of the Sacramento Delta, far from the wide expanses of the Pacific where he belonged. The water was wrong. The scenery was wrong. Humphrey was confused and in deep trouble.

But that's not the end of the story. There was a whale of a lot of sympathy for Humphrey. His plight became headline news around the world. A whale of a lot of money was raised in a hurry to try to help him. A whale of a lot of energy was put forth to get Humphrey back into the Pacific Ocean. A lot of people became involved.

They dredged under bridges so Humphrey could get through. They beat on metal pipes and played music of whales feeding; they herded him along with a flotilla of gunboats and private craft. They cheered as Humphrey finally made his way back under the Golden Gate Bridge and out into the open sea. The whole world joined them in the cheering.

In a way, we are all a bunch of Humphreys. We have all made wrong turns and paid the price in misery, pain, and confusion. Who of us has not turned away from the freedom and joy of God's ocean, the "life more abundant," and ended up wallowing in the muddy waters far from where God wants us to be?

It's scary to think how easy it is to make a wrong turn in life. Just ask Adam, Saul, David, Peter, and yes, Judas. And you might call on the Prodigal Son to give a word of testimony.

What is *really* wonderful is that we can *right* a wrong turn. We can confess our sins, repent, and go back to where God wants us to be. God is fully aware of our wrong turns. We may make wrong turns away from Him, but He never turns away from us. He is always alongside, putting pressure on us to return to where we belong. His promise is loud and clear: "I will never leave you nor forsake you" (Hebrews 13:5).

Humphrey, wherever you are, have a good swim. In a way, I'm glad you made a wrong turn. Thanks for giving me a lesson and a spiritual lift. But I'm even more glad that you are back where you belong.

Bon Voyage!

Dear You

WHY DO ROOSTERS CROW?

Every morning, very *early* every morning, *too* early every morning, I am awakened by the insistent and incessant sound of roosters crowing in the Bird Sanctuary in Marina del Rey across the street from my second story bedroom. The roosters will not be denied. Sometimes I lie there feeling annoyed, but I gradually become amused. Then I start wondering, "Why do roosters crow?"

I have asked several well-educated people that question. They not only did not know the answer, they did not even know anyone who might know. I thought of calling veterinarians with the question, but I thought it would sound kind of ridiculous: "Could you tell me why roosters crow?" Probably someone does have the answer, but I still don't know.

But the World Book Encyclopedia did tell me *how* they crow: "Roosters crow by means of an organ called the syrinx. The syrinx is located at the place where the windpipe splits into the two bronchi. These bronchi are the tubes that carry air into the birds' lungs." (Got it?)

Well, for whatever reason, they do it, and however they *manage* to do it, I know that roosters do crow. And I love to hear them crow.

They seem to be giving a cheery call to the new day. They let me know that even though it is still dark, the sun will soon be rising and the world will soon be lighted up. There's a staccato upbeat to their awakening call. They seem to be glad that there is a new day coming. They seem to be anticipating it.

Not all of them make a pleasant sound. Amidst the cheery crowing there is one rooster whose "voice" invariably brings a grin to my face. He sounds like he has a bad case of laryngitis. He doesn't crow, he croaks. But it is a cheery croak with plenty of volume. Sometimes I think he has given up. But then comes a lull after the others have crowed themselves out, and on he comes again with his croaky rattle. The other roosters have better voices, but old Croaky greets the new day with as much enthusiasm as any of them.

How we all need to look upon each new day as a new adventure, as another gift of twenty-four hours of opportunity from God. We have all had those mornings when we would just like to pull the covers over our heads and forget the whole thing. Many times the misery and the defeats of yesterday make the new day an unavoidable attempt to forget.

That's why I like the cheery crowing of the roosters. They seem to be so excited and so ready for the new day—every day. Especially old Croaky.

Each morning of our lives is so important. It is a new beginning. The start of a new adventure. A new opportunity.

"*This* is the day the Lord hath made; we will *rejoice* and be glad in it" (Psalm 118:24 KJV).

DO WE REALLY BELIEVE IN PRAYER?

Do we *really* believe that God *really* answers prayer? Years ago there was a small town in Kansas which prided itself on the fact there were no establishments that sold liquor in the town. Eventually, however, an enterprising fellow with a sharp eye for a fast buck came along and built a night club right on the main street. The town was shocked. Members of the town's leading church became so upset over what they viewed as a sinful intrusion into the life of their community that they conducted all-night prayer vigils. They fervently prayed that God would somehow put an end to this "den of iniquity."

Amazingly enough, a short time later a bolt of lightning struck the night club. It was totally destroyed!

The night club owner was told that the church members had been praying for the destruction of his club. He sued the church and its members for damages. His attorney claimed that the prayers of the church had caused the loss of the club. The church's attorney, on the other hand, argued that the prayers of the church members had nothing whatever to do with the destruction of the club. Since lightning is legally considered to be an "act of God," the case was eventually thrown out of court.

But the judge, in writing his opinion, made a very pertinent remark: "It is the opinion of this court that wherever the blame lies over the fire, the night club owner apparently is the one who believes in prayer while the church members clearly do not."

Think about that for a minute. It's all too true, isn't it?

Remember the time the disciples were praying for the apostle Peter's release from prison? Their prayers were answered. Peter was released, against all odds. But when he knocked on the door of the building in which the Christians were still praying for his release, the people holding vigil were so startled and surprised, they wouldn't open the door for him. They couldn't believe it—even though they were praying for it!

Perhaps we should be praying this prayer: "Lord, I pray that You will help me to *believe* in prayer."

P.S. "Prayer changes things."

WINDS AND WOODEN LEGS

To see how some people face the "contrary winds of life" is inspiring and encouraging. Rip Sewell, now seventy-nine years of age, with two artificial legs as the result of surgery for a circulatory problem, still plays golf three times a week. He is a good example.

Rip Sewell was a pitcher for the Pittsburgh Pirates many years ago and was famous for a pitch called the "blooper ball." This was a pitch so slow it fooled many of the greatest hitters, who were used to swinging at pitches with much more velocity. He still delights in telling stories about his famous "blooper ball." He says, "Whitey Kurowski of the Cardinals wouldn't swing at it. He'd just spit tobacco juice on it as it went by.

"Eppie Miller of the Reds let one hit him right in the rump. He started toward first base, but George Magerkurth, the umpire, called him back. The umpire said 'Eppie, the rule book says you have to try to get out of the way of the ball, and you had five minutes to get out of the way of that one.'"

Sewell jokes about his wooden legs. "I used to be six-foot one-and-a-half inches tall, but now I'm only six feet. That's because of termites. I have no corns, no bunions or ingrown toenails, and my feet never smell. I just change my socks every six months and spray for termites once a year."

Now that's the way to face adversity, to sail headlong into the "contrary winds" of life.

I never tire of reading about the radiant reaction of Paul and Silas to the inhumane and unjust treatment they received when they brought the gospel to Philippi. After receiving a clear call from God and then faithfully witnessing for Christ, they were falsely accused, severely beaten, thrown into the inner dungeon of the prison, and their hands and feet were put into stocks.

Did they moan about their fate? Did they doubt their call? Did they beg for deliverance? How did they react? "At midnight Paul and Silas prayed, and sang praises unto God" (Acts 16:25 KJV). That's how they reacted!

Our resources determine our reactions. For Paul and Silas, the dungeon was not dark. The "Light of the World" was there with them. For them, joy was "an inside job." They were not situation-oriented, but Savior-oriented. Years later, Paul, writing to the church at Philippi, clued them into his resources: "I can do all things through Christ who strengtheneth me" (Philippians 4:13 KJV).

So can we.

LAUGHTER AND LIVING

I am a laugher. A congenital laugher. For as long as I can remember, things have struck me funny, and, when they do, I cannot resist laughing.

Back in 1923, my parents, my sister, my three brothers and I were motoring from Detroit, Michigan, to Los Angeles. I was then a lad of only eleven years. To our chagrin we had a flat tire in the middle of the Mojave Desert.

With the heat bearing down on us, and with my father deeply concerned, what did I do? I laughed. My stern Scottish dad turned on me and yelled, "What are you laughing at?" I laughed louder. He glared at me for a moment, then his face softened, a grin began to form, and finally he burst out laughing, too. By then, every member of my family was laughing.

I'm so glad the Bible says, "For everything there is a season. . . . a time to weep, and a time to laugh" (Ecclesiastes 3:4).

Charles Haddon Spurgeon, the great English preacher, loved to laugh and to give everyone else a laugh. Some of his deacons thought he carried it too far. They approached him and said, "Mr. Spurgeon, we wish you would not use so much humor in the pulpit." Spurgeon paused for a moment, then replied with a smile, "Gentlemen, if you just knew how much I hold back, you would surely forgive me."

I'm glad the Bible says, "There is a time to laugh."

Dr. Norman Cousins found out that laughing can be lifesaving. He developed a serious illness, usually fatal. His doctors despaired of his recovery and basically sent him home to die. But Cousins absolutely refused to let it be a time of gloom. He had his wife get him all the humorous books and articles available, as well as cartoons and comedy films—anything to make him laugh. He laughed and laughed, but he did not laugh himself to death. He laughed himself to life. He laughed himself back to health. His doctors were astonished. They re-examined him and declared him cured. Cousins wrote a best-selling book about his experience which has helped many others laugh themselves to health. He became a faculty member at the UCLA medical school.

I'm so glad the Bible says, "There is a time to laugh."

Jesus must have known how to laugh. He was invited to, and attended, very happy occasions such as weddings. He certainly was no kill-joy. I'm sure Jesus was Lord of the laugh as well as Lord of the sob.

Yes, of course, there is also "a time to weep," and we are admonished to "weep with those who weep." But we should also "laugh with those who laugh." God wants us to pray, to read the Bible, to witness, to give, and to serve. He wants us to do these things for our own good. And there is something else He wants us to do for our own good—

Have a good belly-laugh!

MUSHROOMS AND KITTENS

Did you ever stop to think about the assumptions we make about people and situations? About how these assumptions affect our lives and the lives of others for good or for bad?

For example: One day a man and his wife went hunting for mushrooms in the country. They were successful and brought home a good supply. Helped by their children, they cleaned the mushrooms, prepared them, and cooked them as part of a full meal. It was a real feast. Being a family of mushroom-lovers, they all ate their fill with great enjoyment. They gave the leftovers to the cat in the kitchen. It gulped down the remains of the feast with like enthusiasm.

Later the same evening, after they had drunk their last cups of coffee, someone went into the kitchen. In obvious pain, the cat was writhing on the floor. A horrible thought struck everybody at once. The cat had obviously gotten sick from eating poisonous mushrooms!

In panic they called the hospital. They were instructed to come to the emergency room immediately. At the hospital, they all had their stomachs pumped. As they returned home, they thought about the poor cat and wondered whether she was still alive. They entered the kitchen. The cat was still lying on the floor.

With three new-born kittens!

This is a funny story, but our assumptions are not always funny. One time I was expressing criticism of a fellow minister because he had not responded when I'd spoken to him. The person I was speaking to replied, "Don, he probably didn't hear you. Did you know that he is almost stone deaf?" A false assumption on my part.

Another time, I was sitting at the counter in a small restaurant, getting ready to order. The waitress seemed brusque and unfriendly. I concluded she was a person with an obviously nasty disposition. When she served my meal, she poured herself a cup of coffee and sat down alongside me. As she sipped her coffee, she began to tell me about how her husband had lost his job, about a very sick child at home, about crushing financial problems and other burdens she was carrying.

How glad I was that I had kept my mouth shut, that I had not made the cutting remarks which had come into my mind on initial contact with this waitress. I had made a false assumption about her. She was not nasty. She was hurting.

It's easy to make false assumptions about people. It is a matter that calls for prayerful humility. And for real sensitivity to the needs, the pains, and the problems of other human beings.

"Man looketh on the outward appearance, but the Lord looketh on the heart" (1 Samuel 16:7 KJV).

LONELINESS AND LIGHT

Over twenty years ago, I found myself in the lonely Room 617 of the Commodore Hotel in downtown Los Angeles. After twenty-seven years of marriage, and with three fine children and all the happy times of family life—there I was, at midnight, in this dusty room overlooking a deserted city, living all alone for the first time in my life. As I lay down on the small bed alongside the wall, I felt a crushing sense of loneliness and an engulfing feeling of worthlessness and failure.

I found that by lying on my right side, I could peer outside the window. I could see the burning torch on top of the Richfield Building. That was a bright spot on my heavy-hearted horizon. Close by was the huge neon sign of the Church of the Open Door. The sign had two lighted words, "JESUS SAVES." All through that lonely night, I looked out, through stinging tears, to those two encouraging supports visible from Room 617.

I couldn't think a single optimistic thought. I couldn't pray. I could just lie there alone. Look out the window. And survive.

I'm sure that when you read this, many of you, in your hearts, will say, "I know, I know what you mean. I've been there, too."

You know what helps most when we feel we are not worth anything? When we feel that we are failures? It is to realize how much we are worth to God despite our personal failures.

After all, we are something special to God. We are not stones or insects. We are created in the very image of God. We have the capacity to think, to feel, and to will.

Above all, God loves us. "God so loved the world that he gave . . ." (John 3:16). At the heart of the universe is a God who loves us. Always before us is the image of the Cross. It is a constant reminder that God thinks we are of infinite worth. The Bible says, ". . . God commendeth his love toward us, in that, while we were yet sinners, Christ died for us" (Romans 5:8 KJV).

A comeback is always available. "As many as received him, to them gave he power to become the sons of God . . ." (John 1:12 KJV). How can you feel worthless when you are a child of God?

When I looked out of Room 617 of the Commodore Hotel on that lonely night many years ago and saw the light of the Richfield torch against the darkness, my heavy heart was encouraged by the words of Jesus, ". . . I am the light of the world . . ." (John 8:12).

I survived.

So can you.

WHO HOLDS THE ROPE?

I'm such a slow learner.

I keep trying to hold onto God instead of letting Him hold onto me. I try to "keep the faith" instead of simply having a faith that is able to keep me. It's so easy to try so hard to be a Christian. Why do I keep trying to hang on when I know I should just "let go"? My grip is not strong enough, or long enough. God's grip is.

Years ago, a party of American tourists was spending some days in the mountainous regions of Scotland. Many people literally risk their lives ascending and descending the precipitous slopes of these beautiful mountains.

The group was particularly interested in the study of rock formations and flowers. One, an enthusiastic botanist, saw some rare flowers on a rock ledge far below. He was eager to obtain some of these flowers, but he could not persuade any member of the group to venture down the steep ledge.

Nearby, a father and son, who, along with their dogs, were guarding sheep, were also observing the tourists. The botanist offered the boy a liberal reward if he would allow a strong rope to be tied around his body so he could be lowered down the clifflike slope to pluck the rare flowers below. The tourists demonstrated to the boy and his father that the rope was strong enough to hold a dozen men. The father gave his consent. But the boy, although he was already an experienced mountain climber, hesitated to accept the offer, though he would have liked very much to earn the money. His fear was made apparent when he looked over to his stalwart father and said, "I'll go if my father will hold the rope."

We are living in a scary world. No matter how loud we turn up the volume on our stereos or television sets or radios, it will not drown out the frightening facts. We have more than enough nuclear power plants and enough hydrogen bombs to

turn the planet Earth into a massive fireball. We have enough men and women in white lab coats tinkering with genetic materials, playing with the possibility of causing disastrous irreversible changes in organic life, even in the human body. We all have, in our own lives, the inescapable and constant potential for unexpected falls and disasters. But, somehow, we can make it through.

"If my FATHER will hold the rope."

CONTRARY WINDS

There was a period of time, a few years ago, when I had gotten out of a long habit of daily running due to some knee problems. I hadn't yet gotten into my present habit of taking long daily walks. As a result, I was getting progressively out of shape—and heavier. My doctor suggested that I try riding a bicycle for exercise.

So, after an approximately fifty-year hiatus from bike riding, I starting riding a bicycle ten miles a day on the bike path alongside the lovely blue Pacific Ocean between Marina del Rey and Santa Monica. I was fearful and wobbly at first, but the more I rode, the less my behind hurt, and the more I grew in balance and confidence.

One day, as I headed north toward my turnaround point at Santa Monica, I found myself going along faster and more effortlessly than ever before. What fun it was! It seemed I hardly had to push the pedals. *Boy, this is great! I never realized that I would get in such good condition so fast. The muscles in my legs must be developing really well,* I thought. I sat straight up on my bike and rode along like a conquering hero. King for a day! Then . . .

Reality struck!

It happened when I turned around to come back. Wham! I was hit in the face with a very brisk wind. To make any forward progress at all, I had to almost stand up on the pedals. Now I knew why I had found it so easy going the other way. The strong wind had been at my back, pushing me along. But now I had a decidedly contrary wind. It was hard going. As I struggled along, making precious little progress, I was tempted to get off and walk the bike back home.

Then a thought struck me. *Hey, you are out here for exercise. Now you are really developing the muscles of your heart, lungs, and legs. It is the wind in your face that brings the most development, not the wind at your back.* So I struggled on and made it back home, not feeling nearly as heroic as I had while going down-wind earlier.

How true to life. Sooner or later we all learn that the wind is not always at our backs. Many times we face contrary winds that try our souls. We feel like quitting. The winds are just too contrary and too strong. But, thank God, out of the hard and gusty winds of disappointment, suffering, sadness, rejection, adversity, and pain, comes the development of our spiritual muscles.

It's fun to have the wind at our backs. But growth comes from having the wind in our face.

New Creatures

"Therefore if any one is in Christ, he is a new creation . . ." (2 Corinthians 5:17).

What a startling affirmation! A *new* creation? Yes, a new creation!

This is especially amazing when you realize how early our lives are conditioned by influences surrounding us and how very early in life we get "set in our ways."

Years ago, my doctor's wife, a registered nurse, told me what happened when she and her husband brought their adopted daughter home from the maternity ward of a local hospital. When night came on, she tucked the baby in bed, turned out the light, and left the room.

But the baby began to cry. Assuming a diaper might be wet, she returned to the bedroom to check. Nope, nice and dry. Again she turned out the light and left. She was barely seated when she once more heard the baby crying. Now what? Then she thought, *Maybe a safety pin has come loose and is sticking the baby.* Back to the bedroom. No, everything was fine. She turned out the lights again and went back to reading the newspaper. But not for long. Another cry. By now she was getting annoyed. *What's going on here?*

She was about to let the baby "cry it out," but her mother's heart said, Well, maybe she has gas on the stomach and needs to burp. So, back to the bedroom once more. She held the baby over her shoulder and patted her back. Nothing happened, so again she put the infant to bed, turned out the lights, and left.

When the baby cried again, she suddenly realized what was happening. For seven days the infant had slept in the maternity ward where there was always a light left on. Now, in her own way, she was registering a complaint, saying, in effect, "Turn on that light!" The doctor's wife returned to the bedroom and turned on a light. When she left the room this time, there was no more crying.

Now, add on years and years of conditioning and you have some kind of idea how "set" our personalities get. In a thousand ways, thousands of influences pound us into a certain shape. The shape of "this world." And the cement gets more solid as the years go by. This is a startling fact.

But there is something far more startling. God can break into the pattern, no matter how solid it is, and completely change the person. Charles Colson, a clever, shrewd and worldly attorney, was sent to prison for breaking the law as a principal in the Watergate scandal. But God broke into the set pattern of Charles Colson. Colson became a Christian, a "new creature." This was a startling experience for him and for everyone who knew him. No wonder Colson could write a book about it, entitled simply—

Born Again.

THE NEEDS OF OTHERS

Each morning I walk down to the beach near my home, then alongside the lovely Pacific Ocean, and finally back home a couple hours or so later. The exercise makes my bulky frame feel better the rest of the day.

Sunday morning is tough. Since our church service begins at 9:30 A.M., I must be headed toward the beach while it is still dark outside.

One Sunday morning, I was puffing and blowing in the predawn darkness when two figures loomed up in front of me. One was a man and the other was a little boy. I paused for a moment and felt a little apprehensive. A number of people have been assaulted on this very street. But this man was holding the hand of the little boy who stood alongside him. Bundled up in heavy clothing, the man looked at me with clear blue eyes and said, "You wouldn't have a cigarette, would you?"

It caught me completely off balance. I gave a ridiculous reply. I mumbled, "I'm sorry to say, I don't." It sounded as if I was sorry I didn't smoke. I thought I heard the man say, "I thought so," as he turned and headed down the sidewalk, knapsack slung over his shoulder, holding the hand of the small boy who toddled along at his side. It was a pathetic picture. When I glanced back a minute later, they were gone.

As I continued my trip to the end of the pier, questions flooded my mind. Why were these two up so early on this raw morning? Was the little boy the man's son? What were the events that caused them to be in such a condition?

On my return trip I looked for them as I passed by the same place, but they had vanished. Then other questions began to bother me. I wondered if the man had enough money to buy himself and the boy some breakfast. Was the boy physically well? Did the dad—or whoever the man was—need some help?

But I had to hurry on home, shave, shower, dress, and put the finishing touches on my sermon for the morning.

Perhaps you might like to know the title of my sermon— "BEING SENSITIVE TO THE NEEDS OF OTHERS."

A Sermon from Sparrows

When I was in Honolulu a few years ago, I got a sermon from some sparrows. I was having breakfast in the outdoor section of the dining room at the Reef Hotel on a lovely morning. A swarm of sparrows was flitting around the vines that circled the dining room.

I tossed a few pieces of bread on the patio. Instantly, the sparrows flew down and began busily pecking away at the bread. I kept throwing the bread closer and closer to me, and the sparrows kept coming closer and closer. Finally, I put a piece of bread in my hand and held it out. To my happy surprise, several of those little gray sparrows landed on my hand and pecked away at the bread.

It gave me a nice feeling. It was comforting to have the trust of these little creatures. Why did they come so close? Because they were not afraid of getting hurt. These sparrows were literally putting their lives in my hand. At any moment I could have closed my hand and crushed them. Their trust had put them at my mercy.

As I say, I got a sermon from those sparrows. Actually, it's a prayer: "Lord, help me to treat people in such a loving way that they will not be afraid to come close—that they will not be afraid they will get hurt."

We need to pray that prayer because we have all been hurt, and we have all hurt other people close to us. So many people have come close with a trusting heart of love only to be hurt with criticism, betrayal, and rejection. How many of us have had our confession turned into a club? A sin against love is the worst kind.

But the sparrows took a chance. They felt the bread was worth the risk.

I am reminded of the old saying, "It is better to have loved and lost than never to have loved at all." A close relationship of love is worth the risk. A real fellowship with God and others demands a relationship based on love. The joy and happiness available to us all can only come in that way. It does not come to spectators.

It only comes to *participants*.

THROW SOMEONE A LINE

I stood on the Venice Pier and watched anxiously as two fishermen in their twenty-foot boat drifted dangerously close to the heavy surf. A few more feet and the boat would be tossed on the shore by the crashing waves. The two men on board were obviously unable to start their outboard engine despite their frantic efforts. The situation seemed hopeless.

Then I heard the voice of a young lifeguard booming out of a bullhorn from the lifeguard truck that had pulled up on the shore. The lifeguard shouted out, "You are not allowed to come within two hundred yards of the shore." There was no response from the boat. "Skipper, start your engine!" Again, no response. The lifeguard yelled, "If you can hear me, wave your arms." Both men on board waved their arms vigorously.

That did it. The two lifeguards, one a young lady, sprang out of the yellow truck, grabbed their lifelines and plunged into the turbulent surf. I stood tensely watching from the rail of the pier as they ducked under the waves and furiously stroked their way toward the stricken boat. My heart was warmed as I watched the tanned bodies of these two caring and dedicated people as they splashed their way through the chilling morning waters of the blue Pacific.

Knowing just what to do, they never hesitated. The female lifeguard swam to the front of the boat, attached her lifeline to the boat, and then started swimming out to sea with the heavy boat in tow. By now, the male lifeguard had attached his lifeline, too, and was also in front trying to tow the boat away from shore. The boat had drifted in to the point at which it could easily have been caught by a huge wave and tossed on the shore.

Was it too late? Was this heroic effort in vain?

I held my breath and watched. The two lifeguards were swimming furiously, their lines tugging at the heavy boat. The

boat had stopped drifting toward the shore. Then, little by little, the boat began to move slowly away from the dangerous surf and out into safer waters.

Hurrah! They did it! In my heart, I cheered them. I thanked God for them.

The lifeboat, *The Baywatch,* sped around the pier and took the boat in tow toward the Marina. The two lifeguards swam wearily back to shore. Reluctantly, they gave me their names, Anne Philpott and Louis Chao. Now, you can be thankful for them too.

This beautiful example of caring makes me want to be more caring. All around us there are people who are drifting in dangerous waters. They need someone to attach a line of love to them and give them a tow into safer waters.

Give someone a line.

MY HEARING PROBLEM

One day a woman, not known for her timidity, blurted out to me bluntly, "You have a hearing problem. You don't know it, but you miss a lot of what is being said. You should go see a hearing specialist."

I gave her a tolerant look and brushed off her remark as being rather rude.

A short time later, a very close friend put it in the form of a question, "Do you have a hearing problem?" Trying to be cute, but evasive, I replied, "I was able to hear what you just said. Ha! Ha!"

Even before anybody said anything about it, I had begun to notice that I was enjoying programs and lectures much more when I was close to the front of the room. Sometimes an audience would laugh at a speaker's joke, and I would wonder what was so funny. I noticed that when people spoke to me they often mumbled their words. I lamented the fact that so many people these days have not learned to speak clearly as we were taught when I was a kid. *Enunciation, nowadays, is just terrible,* I thought. *Even the phones aren't what they used to be. You can barely make out what people are saying. It causes me to get numbers and names mixed up sometimes.*

But despite these problems in my environment, I knew that my hearing was really quite all right.

Nevertheless, to satisfy everyone else, I went to a topnotch hearing specialist and had a thorough examination. The doctor said, plainly enough for me to hear him distinctly, "You have some hearing loss."

But that is not my *main* hearing problem. My main hearing problem is that, so often, I do not hear what God is trying to say to me.

Oh, yes, I do read the Bible, but I don't always hear what

the Author is saying to my heart. The clamor of "this world" is so noisy I cannot hear the "still, small voice" of God.

I talk too much. I don't listen enough. One cannot do both at the same time. I need to humbly pray, "Lord, heal my spiritual hearing problem. I really do want to hear what You have to say about salvation, about the 'abundant life,' about the reality of heaven. Lead me to the nearest off-ramp from the fast and noisy freeway of this life so that I can hear Your Voice speaking to my heart."

Loud and clear.

Are you listening?

CONTENTMENT

How many contented people do you know? Are you one of them?

How many times have you heard people use the word "if" when it comes to contentment: *If* I had better health. *If* I had a better job. *If* I were living in a different area. *If* I had an understanding wife. *If* I had a considerate husband. *If* I had more money. *If* people would be more accepting of me. *If* people would just appreciate me. *If* my children would just show more love. *If* my parents would only have more understanding?

The list is endless.

The person with this attitude is programmed for failure. He will never be a really contented person because he is basing his happiness on external circumstances. Contentment is always contingent. The internal is always dependent on the external.

But it won't work. Joy is an inside job.

The apostle Paul made this discovery. Listen to him: "Not that I complain of want; for I have learned, in whatever state I am, to be *content*. . . . I can do all things in him who strengthens me" (Philippians 4:11, 13).

Paul learned to be content while worshiping with fellow Christians and while being held prisoner in a dungeon. He could be happy when he was sailing along in a boat and when he was clinging to a piece of debris in the open sea. He was contented when he had lots of food and contented when he had scarcely any food.

Paul had learned a great secret, the secret of not depending on external circumstances. His joy was an inside job.

And you and I can learn what the apostle Paul learned. And it is, indeed, a *learning* process. We need to learn it every day. One day at a time. We can never *learn* contentment if we continually *lean* on circumstances, and on other people, to make us happy.

Abraham Lincoln once said, "A man is just about as happy as he makes up his mind to be." That is to say, happiness comes from the inside, not from the outside.

Above all, remember the energy source we have available. Paul says he could be content in all circumstances *because* Christ gave him the strength to do so. "I can do all things through Christ who strengthens me."

Contentment is still available. Christ is still available.

Take both.

THE STRESS TEST

A few years ago, Dr. William Corey, a highly respected internist and my own personal doctor for over twenty years, gave me my annual physical exam, including an electrocardiogram. He was very pleased with the results. He said I was physically fit and my heart was working well.

However, since my brother, Adam, had died of a heart attack recently, and my brother, Doug, had to have an emergency coronary by-pass operation, Dr. Corey said he thought I should undergo the "Stress Test" for my heart, just to be on the cautious side. So with great confidence in my heart's condition, I took the Stress Test at the Huntington Memorial Hospital in Pasadena.

A few days later, Dr. Corey gave me the report. He also gave me a shock. My heart had failed the Stress Test. There was insufficient blood supply to my heart. I had a strong enough heart for normal living but not for stressful living. I could get by for routine activities but not for maximum exertion. I felt fine but my heart was becoming a ticking time bomb. I never would have guessed it.

The Stress Test made the difference.

After receiving the report, I sat in stunned silence. I couldn't believe it. For many years I had jogged or cycled or walked on a daily basis. Is this what I get for all that diligent exercise? It isn't fair. How could this happen to me?

Gradually I came to accept the truth and to prepare myself mentally for by-pass surgery. Then, as I worked my way out of depression, a spiritual message began to emerge . . .

The Stress Test makes the difference.

Our spiritual lives must be strong enough to face the Stress Test because the stresses of life will surely come. The stresses of loneliness, of temptation, of rejection, of fear of death, of fear of life, of ruptured relationships, of sickness, of pain, and of disillusionment. These stresses can be just too much for a weak spiritual heart, but they are inevitable, eventually, for all of us. We must all, ultimately, face the Stress Test of life, no matter how easily and comfortably things seem to be riding along at present.

Like the man in the Bible who knew that storms would be coming, and, therefore, built his house upon a rock, we must build our own lives with the inescapable storms always in mind. The Stress Test is always on the horizon, and a phony faith will never pass the Stress Test. Remember this—a person's faith is no stronger than his hardest test.

The apostle Paul was able to pass the Stress Test. Listen to him: ". . . I have learned how to get along happily whether I have much or little. I know how to live on almost nothing or with everything. I have learned the secret of contentment in every situation, whether it be a full stomach or hunger, plenty or want; for I can do everything God asks me to with the help of Christ who gives me the strength and power" (Philippians 4:11–13 TLB).

Are *you* ready for the Stress Test?

ALWAYS THANKFUL

One Sunday morning not long ago, I preached on these words from the Bible: "Always be joyful. Always keep on praying. No matter what happens, always be thankful, for that is God's will for you who belong to Christ Jesus" (1 Thessalonians 5:16–17 TLB).

The following week my Associate Pastor at the Church of the Marina, Bill Douglas, was driving serenely along the Santa Monica Freeway when he was startled by a loud scraping sound under his car. He coasted to the side of the freeway as quickly as he could, got out and looked under the car. It was not a pretty sight; the driveshaft was hanging down on the pavement.

Then, Bill, remembering the words I had preached on—"No matter *what* happens, always be thankful"—turned to his wife inside the car and said, "Well, I guess I just have to say, Praise the Lord!"

To be sure, a major breakdown on the freeway is not the *worst* possible crisis in life, but it may be one of the most annoying. I'm sure it wasn't easy for Bill to respond with thanksgiving of any sort. It's not easy for any of us, when things go very wrong, to actually practice "thanksgiving" instead of self-pity or anger or frustration.

It's so easy to say instead, "Why me?" "Why this?" "Why now?" It is maddening to have negative interruptions in our "game plan" for life.

When things "come apart at the seams" in our lives, as they sometimes do, invariably it is the most "natural" thing in the world to react with bitterness. That is the "knee-jerk reaction." But anger, resentment, and bitterness are never the way to joy and happiness. That route is downhill all the way.

Thankfulness, regardless of the circumstances, is the only way to go. Listen to God's Word again, *"No matter what happens, always* be thankful, for this is the will of God for you." This is God's way. This is God's will.

Thanking God for everything, regardless of the circumstances, is "positive thinking" at the divine level. It is not mere wishful thinking for verbal bravado.

Thanking God for everything that happens is a joyous act of faith. It is a recognition that "all things work together for good to them that love the Lord." It is an affirmation that, in *all* circumstances, "Underneath are the everlasting arms."

Joyfulness and thankfulness go together. You can't have one without the other.

"Count your blessings, name them one by one,/and it will surprise you what the Lord has done."

"I DON'T KNOW WHERE I AM"

In 1985, the whole world was put into a state of shock when a Boeing airplane, carrying 525 holiday passengers between Tokyo and Osaka, crashed into a mountain in the "Japanese Alps." Only four people survived. The last words of the captain were pathetic in their finality.

"Unable to control."

"I don't know where I am."

For thirty-nine tense minutes, the Air Traffic Controllers in Tokyo had watched and listened as the huge aircraft had wandered about on the radar screen. Then, all at once, complete silence. At the same time the plane disappeared from the radar screen. A short time later other aircraft sighted the crash in the mountains.

Questions flew quickly. Why would a sophisticated plane, with all the latest guidance equipment, piloted by a seasoned veteran with thousands of hours of flying time, go completely out of control and leave the pilot completely lost? With five complete backup guidance systems, how could such a thing happen?

Overwhelming evidence came from the debris and from the testimony of the four survivors. The tall vertical stabilizer in the tail section of the plane had disintegrated, leaving the plane unstable and uncontrollable. The pilot became a victim of forces beyond his control. He was therefore helpless and lost.

And so are we all helpless and lost if God is not the Stabilizer in our lives. In a world of life-threatening mountan peaks, we all must have an indestructible Stabilizer or we will surely wander about, out of control. And we will ultimately crash. A human stabilizer is not enough. We must have a Stabilizer linked to the Infinite: infinite strength, infinite wisdom, infinite love, infinite guidance, infinite security. And, above all, infinitely inseparable.

In short, if we are going to stay on course and not get lost, God must be our indestructible and ever-present Stabilizer. He promises: "*God* is our refuge and strength, a very present help in trouble" (Psalm 46:1).

THE UNSINKABLE

I have just read the story of Shackleton's incredible voyage to the South Pole in 1914, the same year World War One began in Europe. What a gripping tale it is, an account of courage and human endurance in the face of the unforgivingly cold and brutally strong winds in that remote and frozen region of the world.

After their wooden ship, *Endurance*, was crushed by the Antarctic ice, Shackleton and his brave men were forced to survive by living in their little tents on windswept "ice floes." Ultimately, each of these floes upon which they would make their "home" for a time would break up, and they would have to scramble frantically onto another floe. In the end, they ran out of floes and had to climb into the three small boats they had salvaged from the *Endurance*. Then, in these tiny vessels, they faced all the terrors of the turbulent Antarctic Ocean.

What a gallant fight they put up to stay alive. For many days, they rode the high waves and frigid winds of the open sea. They withstood Antarctic blizzards hunkered down within their tiny boats, mere specks of wood against the dark, angry sea. In the cold, cramped quarters of these small boats, they were constantly shivering and, in some cases, hands and feet became frozen. There was nothing they could do but shake, hope, huddle together, and wonder. Many of them were sick, but they sailed and rowed, whenever they could, in the direction of Elephant Island.

Then, one day, it happened! One of the men, peering through the mist, thought he saw something. He took a long, hard, intensive look at the horizon. Then he shouted out, in sheer delight, "Land!"

All eyes strained to see. Sure enough, there it was. Rising from the sea, there were the 3500-foot peaks of Elephant Island dead ahead in the distance. Excitement warmed the hearts of these tired and worn-out men as they carefully steered their little boats toward the island. Before too long, the bottoms of their boats were scraping onto the rocky shore.

Historian Alfred Lansing writes: "They were on land.

"It was the merest handhold, one hundred feet wide and fifty feet deep, a meager grip on a savage coast exposed to the full fury of the Antarctic Ocean. But no matter—they were on land. For the first time in 497 days, they were on land.

"Solid, unsinkable, immovable, blessed land!"

This is the experience of the person who has become a Christian. He has been blown around by the cold and contrary winds of life, and he has felt the frightening feelings of insecurity and instability. He has wandered from one ice floe to another and sailed his frail boat in the open sea. Then he finds Christ! He has found *the* solid foundation. He can say for the first time, "I have found solid, unsinkable, immovable, blessed land!"

THE UNHAPPY ENDING

The last days of Jesus' life on this earth were not pleasant ones. They were, in fact, filled with the most intense misery, rejection, punishment, loneliness, and agony.

There was plenty of action in those final days. But all of it was bad. There was the fear and flight of His trusted disciples, His own nighttime arrest at the hands of the Jewish authorities, the kiss of death from Judas, the false accusations against Him, the anger and jealously of the religious leaders, the spitting and punching of the guards, the hysterical screams of the mob clamoring for His crucifixion, and, then, at last, the gruesome death on the cross.

No, it was not a pleasant ending to the most beautiful life ever lived on this earth. That such a life could come to such an ending demonstrated the sinfulness of sin.

But out of this tragedy, triumph shone through. Jesus gave a greater demonstration. He demonstrated that a person totally surrendered to God's will and plan can have a majestic composure when everyone—and everything—else is breaking up.

Jesus demonstrated His willingness to accept loneliness for the sake of those He loved. Alone, He prayed in Gethsemane. Alone, He remained after seeing His beloved disciples all run away. Alone, He faced the hostile enemies with their swords and staves. Alone, He suffered the insults of the hypocritical religious leaders. Alone, He took the punches and spit of the cruel guards. Alone, He gave his life.

Again, there is a triumph over tragedy. He accepted all this loneliness and all this abuse so that all who accept Him as their Savior and Lord will never be lonely again. As He promises, ". . . Lo, I am with you always . . ." (Matthew 28:20).

Above all, Jesus demonstrated that God loves us. Behind it all is the love of God. In this painful and graphic scenario, written in divine blood, God is saying in His unforgettable way, "I love you."

He makes it wonderfully clear that we are worth everything to Him. How we need to know that. Sometimes we get so disgusted with ourselves. We feel so inadequate, so worthless. But here is the clincher: if we are worth that much to God, then we certainly must be worth something to ourselves. That's the spiritual vitamin pill we need. We are now "sons of God."

"But as many as received him, to them gave he power to become the sons of God . . ." (John 1:12 KJV).

FALSE GODS

Idolatry must go. We cannot "serve God and mammon." We cannot worship the God of the heavens and also worship at the feet of man-made gods. Spiritual disaster is the immediate result when we try to create God in man's image. God is God. God is the Creator—not man. But the call of the gods of secularism and sensualism are attractive and relentless. It is very easy to be a "conformer" to "this world."

Many years ago, in the Ancient World, the Emperor Theodosius commanded the demolition of a certain heathen temple. Theophilus, a bishop, accompanied by a group of Roman soldiers, hastened to carry out the Emperor's order. They entered the temple where there was a tall image staring down at them. For a moment, the sight of this huge, man-made god, worshiped faithfully by so many people, caused them to pause. Then the bishop shouted out an order for a soldier to strike the image without delay. Hatchet in hand, the soldier made a mighty swing and hit the statue in the knee.

Everyone waited with anticipation. Emotion ran high. But there was neither sound nor sign of divine anger. So, feeling encouraged, the soldier next climbed to the head of this idolatrous image and struck it off. The head rolled down and crashed on the temple floor. A large family of rats, disturbed in their formerly tranquil abode within the sacred image, poured out from the trembling statue and scurried all over the temple floor.

The people in the temple began to laugh. Soon they joined in the destruction of the image. They dragged the fragments of the fallen god through the streets. Even the pagans were disgusted with a god who would not defend himself.

So the huge edifice was completely destroyed and a Christian church was built on the same site. Some people were afraid that the nearby Nile River would show displeasure by refusing its annual innundation, but the river rose with more than the normal fullness and bounty. Every anxiety was gradually dispelled.

Listen to Psalm 115:

> Our God is in the heavens;
>   he does whatever he pleases.
> Their idols are silver and gold,
>   the work of men's hands.
> They have mouths, but do not speak;
>   eyes, but do not see.
> They have ears, but do not hear;
>   noses, but do not smell.
> They have hands, but do not feel;
>   feet, but do not walk;
> And they do not make a sound in their throat.
> Those who make them are like them;
> So are all who trust in them (vv. 3–8).

Oh, God, forgive me for worshiping false gods, and help me to seek first the kingdom of God and His righteousness.
Right now.

ON MAKING EXCUSES

I shall never forget an incident that happened many years ago when I was a seminary student and young father. My wife, Vivian, and I returned home one evening to find little scraps of paper scattered all over the front room carpet. The culprit was my little son, Don. Vivian scolded him and demanded that he pick up all the little scraps from the floor. But Don raised his two small fists and exclaimed, "I can't, Mommy, my hands are stuck." Vivian repeated her demand very forcefully. Finally, little Don, still keeping his fists tightly clenched, started picking up the scraps of paper he'd strewn on the floor. We watched him as he laboriously poked away with his fists until the bits of paper were all picked up. Not once did he unclench his fists, not for a second. He stuck with his excuse. His hands were stuck.

Jesus tells a story to illustrate how adults make excuses:

A man prepared a great feast and sent out many invitations. When all was ready, he sent his servant around to notify the guests that it was time for them to arrive. But they *all* began making excuses. One said he had just bought a field and wanted to inspect it, and he asked to be excused. Another said he had just bought five pair of oxen and he wanted to try them out. Another had just been married and for that reason couldn't come. When the servant reported these excuses to his master, the master made this sober reply, "None of those I invited first will get even the smallest taste of what I had prepared for them" (Luke 14:16–24 TLB).

I don't know why these men did not want to go to the feast prepared for them. But I do know that the reasons they gave for not going were false. They were lies and the men knew it. No matter how plausible we make our excuses, *we* know that they are excuses, and deep down in our guts we can never really excuse our excuses. We are liars and we know it. We project our phony selves into everyone else. We start to assume that everyone else is really a liar making excuses. After all, we tend to think, other people are no different than we are. Everyone becomes suspect—even God.

Reality can only return with confession. Healing starts the minute we say, "I'm sorry, it was my fault; I am to blame." We can go from there. And we can grow from there. But we can never be healed until we admit that we are "sick." To make excuses is to merge fantasy and fact.

We can never enjoy the spiritual banquet God has prepared for us as long as we make excuses.

Dear You

ALCATRAZ

Not long ago I visited Alcatraz Island Federal Prison in the Bay of San Francisco. It is now a museum. But for most of this century it was a prison fortress and a place feared by serious offenders, even the most rough and violent. Here, on this rocky, twelve-acre island, cooped up in five-by-nine-by-seven foot cells, three hundred of the most hardened criminals in the United States were imprisoned.

These men were counted twenty times a day; they were given only twenty minutes to eat each meal; and they were marched single file to and from their tiny cells at the sound of a whistle. That was the routine, three hundred and sixty-five days a year.

It was one prisoner to a cell. Each cell had a steel bed, a sink, a toilet, a fold-out table, a small chair, and a mattress crammed into it. The guards kept constant watch. They were ever-present, even at night. The men were counted at 12:00 A.M., 3:00 A.M., and 5:00 A.M. The slightest infraction of the rules sent a prisoner to "the hole." Any leftover food on a man's plate cost him his next meal.

All freedom was gone! Every sound and sight in this gloomy place was a painful reminder of that oppressive reality. For many of those men, freedom had been lost *forever* by the time they were sent to "the rock."

After going through the depressing interior and feeling the smothering held-in-ness of the bars and the concrete and the steel doors, I stood outside the prison and looked at the lovely shoreline of San Francisco, a scant mile and a half away. To the west, I could see the majestic arc of the Golden Gate Bridge soaring overhead.

I thought to myself, what torture it must have been for these men to be held prisoner on this barren little island in the middle of this gorgeous bay. I thought of how, at night, they could see the bright lights of San Francisco and how they must have hungered for the delights and the fun and the freedom that were out there, a mere 2,625 yards away.

In my imagination, I was so captured by these thoughts and pictures that for a moment I was an agonizing prisoner at infamous Alcatraz. I felt a spasm of depression. An instant of panic. A sense of captivity. A loss of freedom.

Then reality struck me. *I am not a prisoner here, just a visitor. I'll be leaving soon. I am free. I can get on that boat down there and be on my way back to San Francisco. I don't have to go back to a cramped cell. I don't have to be watched by guards. I am free!*

A great surge of joy filled my soul. My, it feels so good to be free. Really free! A whole new appreciation of freedom enveloped me.

Above all, I came away from Alcatraz with a heartfelt gratitude that Christ has made us free. ". . . free from the law of sin and death" (Romans 8:2).

Hurray for the apostle Paul when he says, "For freedom Christ has set us *free;* stand fast therefore . . ." (Galatians 5:1).

Dear You

"Blest Be the Tie That Binds"

For over two hundred years, Christian people, with their hearts full of emotion, have sung, "Blest Be the Tie That Binds." In our own church, oftentimes tearfully, we have sung this lovely hymn at the close of our Communion Service.

The song began in tears. Dr. John Fawcett was the beloved pastor of a small church at Wainsgate, England. In 1772 he received a "call" to become the pastor of a large church in London. He accepted the call from this prestigious church in the capital city of England and preached his farewell sermon to a congregation of crushed and sorrowing parishioners.

The scheduled day of departure arrived. Outside the parsonage, the waiting wagons were loaded up with books, furniture, and other goods of the pastor and his wife. Finally all preparations were complete, and the pastor and his wife were ready to depart. The members of the congregation, who had truly become like "family" to the Fawcetts, gathered around the couple. In a sincere outpouring of affection and emotion, and with eyes full of tears, the people begged them to stay.

The pastor's wife looked at him and with quavering voice said, "Oh, John, John, I cannot bear this."

"Neither can I," exclaimed the good pastor, "and we will not go. Unload the wagons and put everything as it was before."

The pastor's decision brought shouts of joy and thanksgiving from all present. The whole congregation joined in a great, spontaneous celebration.

In commemoration of this touching event, Dr. John Fawcett wrote the words of this hymn:

> Blest be the tie that binds
>   Our hearts in Christian love;
> The fellowship of kindred minds
>   Is like to that above.

Before our Father's throne
  We pour our ardent prayers;
Our fears, our hopes, our aims are one,
  Our comforts and our cares.

We share our mutual woes,
  Our mutual burdens bear;
And often for each other flows
  the sympathizing tear.

When we asunder part,
  It gives us inward pain;
But we shall still be joined in heart,
  And hope to meet again.

What a wonderful tie there is that binds us together in Christian love. It has been my privilege to meet with Christians from all over the world, and always there has been that wonderful "oneness."

"Blest be the tie that binds."

TRUSTING THE TIDE

Several years ago there was a surprising newsflash: The *Enterprise*, a 90,000-ton nuclear-powered aircraft carrier, got stuck in the mud for over five hours on its way into port in San Francisco Bay. The stately 1,123 foot vessel, with a crew of over 5,000 aboard, ran aground just over a thousand yards from the dock.

Thousands of relatives and friends waited on the dock in disbelief as the great ship lurched to a complete halt and then refused to budge. Only a thousand yards from the carrier, people watched eagerly and helplessly as the tugboats were called in to drag the *Enterprise* from the sand bar. The tugs pushed and pulled in all directions. But to no avail. There was shouting of orders and scurrying about, and more tugboats were brought in to "gang up" on the huge ship. They tried everything. The ship would not budge.

The crowd of relatives and friends on the dock looked on this spectacle with increasing frustration and anger. How could such a thing happen? Why couldn't they free the ship? Tension was mounting both on the ship and on the shore.

Then, when everybody was at the end of his rope, help came from another source . . . the tide!

As the high tide began to gradually roll in, it lifted that huge ship right out of the mud where it had been stuck fast for five hours, resisting all human efforts to free it. The silent and powerful lift of the tide—with no help from man—solved the problem.

How many times in life have we got ourselves stuck in the mud? Then we push and pull, we struggle, we wrack our brains. But we find that, despite all our mighty efforts, we are still stuck.

But when God's spiritual tide comes in, we are powerfully and effortlessly lifted free to sail on again. There are times when we need to ". . . stand firm, and see the salvation of the Lord . . ." (Exodus 14:13). We need to remember that it is ". . . not by might, nor by power, but by my Spirit, says the Lord of hosts" (Zechariah 4:6).

"Man's extremity is God's opportunity."

Lord, help me to quit struggling. Help me to learn to trust in the tide.

"Do You Need Assistance?"

I was enjoying the deep sea to the fullest. We were several miles off the Pacific coast, near El Segundo, on a nice, sunny morning with a jovial bunch of men and women happily hoping that a fish would "strike" on their lines.

No one seemed to be catching anything at this location, so Captain Bob Porter of the *Del Mar* yelled, "Haul 'em up," and turned the boat away from shore and out to sea.

As we headed further out to sea, we were confronted with a startling sight. Out in the wide open sea, several hundred yards off to the port side, bobbing in the cold water in a bright orange lifejacket, was a young man in obvious distress. We yelled out to the Captain and crowded the bow. Captain Porter immediately steered the boat toward the young man. As we drew near to the bobbing figure in the water, Captain Porter called out, "Do you need assistance?"

The young man responded by splashing his way to the stern of our boat. Since he was too weak to pull himself aboard, several of us caught hold of him and slid him onto the deck. He was in bad shape, suffering from hypothermia. He mumbled to us that his buddy was in their little boat farther out to sea. Apparently, when their engine failed, this man had tried to swim ashore for help.

We piled coats, jackets, sacks, and everything we could find, on top of him to try to warm him up. A radio call from our boat brought assurance from the lifeguard station that their boat was on its way at full speed. We headed further out to sea to try to find the small boat. A small white spot on the horizon turned out to be it. Its worried and lonely occupant was still aboard and mighty glad to see us approaching. Right then, the speedy lifeboat caught up with us.

The first concern was, of course, for the life of the young man we had on the *Del Mar*. After assuring the man in the stranded boat that another boat was on the way to tow him in, the men in the lifeboat took the young man suffering from hypothermia from our cradled arms and put him on the deck of their boat. They immediately covered him with heavy blankets, gave him oxygen, and tenderly ministered to him as they raced back toward the Marina and the hospital. All of us aboard the *Del Mar* were emotionally drained from the ordeal. Somehow, fishing didn't seem all that important.

Time has gone by, but I can still see that pale young man, helpless and hurting, as he was tossed around in the huge, lonely ocean. God, I'm glad we found him. God, I'm glad we were able to help him.

It makes me think of others, all around us, who are helpless and hurting as they are tossed about by the turbulent sea of life. How they need for someone to come alongside and lovingly call out—

"Do you need assistance?"

"He Came to Himself"

". . . he came to himself . . ." (Luke 15:17).

This was the finest hour in the life of the "Prodigal Son." We are familiar with this young man who, bored with life on the farm, took what he had coming and headed for "a far country." There, he followed pleasure wherever it led him. He blew his money on a "swinging" lifestyle, indulging himself with riotous living, booze, and prostitutes.

Then came the crash! He was broke. What had seemed to him like such a substantial inheritance was already all gone. Not only that, a famine had hit the country. Times were hard. His freeloading friends left him all alone. He then began to realize that after a long run of "high living," he was now in real trouble.

But trouble or no, he had to eat. In desperation, the young man literally pushed himself on a farmer to get the humiliating job of feeding the pigs. But as he ate the pig-food for survival, and as he sloshed around in the muck of the pig pens, something significant happened in the mind of this young derelict.

"He came to himself."

He began to think of where he was and where he had been before. He compared his present lifestyle—that had ended in a pig pen—with the life he'd had at home with his family. He didn't try to defend himself, to justify himself, to kid himself, or to avoid himself.

The Prodigal Son's real, spiritual self looked his worldly, phony self in the eye, and said, "That kind of self has got to go. It has messed up my life, separated me from my father and my home, and brought me to a pig-pen existence."

He immediately confessed his sins. Just as immediately, he was on his way home to a joyous welcome by a loving and forgiving father who had been waiting for him all the while.

The wandering experience of the Prodigal Son is a very real experience in this world. All of us, today, are candidates for wandering. It was never more true that "the grass looks greener" somewhere else. It is all too easy to believe that happiness is waiting for us "out there" in some "far country," some other job, some other marriage, some other neighborhood, some other group of friends, some other way of living. That is simply the continuous and relentless message of "this world."

If you are alive and breathing, you will surely feel the pressures from this society to be a self-satisfying, pleasure-seeking, and self-centered person. But when we reflect in our lives, instead, on such qualities as love, joy, kindness, other-centeredness, and godliness, then people will say of us—"He came to himself."

RECONCILIATION

The father in the hospital waiting room was shocked, delighted, and happy when the doctor told him his wife had given birth to two healthy young boys, identical twins.

As the boys grew up, it was difficult for even their mother to tell one from the other. They looked alike, dressed alike, acted alike, played alike, and talked alike. They liked the same sports, the same studies, the same friends, and the same foods. Unlike some twins, there was virtually no jealously between them. They loved and admired each other. They were inseparable. In the very small town where they lived, both boys were loved and respected by all.

The twins' father, noticing that the small populace of the town had to go away from town to purchase food and other necessities, opened up a general store in the center of town. It was an instant success. People came in not only to buy but to visit and talk. It became the town meeting place. As the twin brothers grew up, they worked in the store with their dad until he died, and then they assumed full responsibility for running the store.

One day a customer made a one dollar purchase, put his dollar bill on the counter, and left the store. The twin serving the man left the dollar on the counter while he went back to the storeroom to get an item. When he returned to the counter, the dollar bill was gone. When he saw his twin brother, he asked him, "Did you put the dollar that was on the counter into the cash register?" The twin replied, "I never saw a dollar on the counter." Many different versions of this same conversation took place. The first twin became increasingly suspicious of his brother, and the brother became more and more defensive and resentful.

Despite the seeming triviality of this incident, and the sum of money involved, a terribly dissonant chord had been struck in the relationship between the twins. Suspicion turned into accusation. The accusations and denials created bitterness. The conflict turned into a verbal civil war.

Word of the dispute between these formerly inseparable brothers spread through the small town. People took sides. Everyone got involved. Positions became intractable.

Finally, in anger, the twins built a wall down the middle of the store. From then on, each stayed in his own half of the store. They lived like this until they were both old men, still filled with hatred for each other.

The twin who had accused his brother was in his side of the store one day when a well-dressed man entered the store. The man said, "I am a Christian, and I've felt guilty about something I want to make right. Many years ago, broke and hungry, I came to this store for help. No one was in the store, but there was a dollar bill on the counter. I took it to get something to eat, then I ran out of the store. Now I've come to pay it back."

Fighting back his tears, the twin said, "Please, go tell that story to the man next door."

The man repeated the story to the other twin. The bitterness and malice of many years disappeared in an instant. The two old men wept as they embraced.

Lord, keep us free of hatred and the desire for retaliation. Give us loving hearts that will always seek reconciliation.

". . . first be reconciled to thy brother, and then come and offer thy gift" (Matthew 5:24 KJV).

WHAT IS A TEARDROP?

What is a "teardrop"?

The dictionary says a teardrop is "a drop of saline fluid secreted by the lachrymal gland."

You may not know much about the lachrymal gland. Neither do I. But you and I both know that a teardrop is much more than a drop of water with salt in it. A teardrop represents our human capacity to feel so deeply with others that tears fill our eyes spontaneously. The capacity to cry represents the capacity to care.

It seems to me that it is much more magnificent to "weep with those that weep" than to "laugh with those that laugh." We should do both, of course, but to "laugh with those that laugh" doesn't cost us anything. On the other hand, to "weep with those that weep" comes only at the cost of hurt-sharing. It costs and it hurts, but, oh, how helpful it can be. Both for the weeper and for the wept-with.

The story was anonymously told of a little girl who came home from a neighbor's house where her little friend had recently died.

Her father questioned her, "Why did you go?"

"To comfort my friend's mother," said the child.

"What could you do to comfort her?"

The little girl said tenderly, "I climbed into her lap and cried with her."

No wonder Jesus said, "Suffer the little children to come unto me, and forbid them not; for of such is the kingdom of God" (Mark 10:14 KJV). And again, "Except ye be converted, and become as little children, ye shall not enter the kingdom of heaven" (Matthew 18:3 KJV).

I would suggest that none of us enters the kingdom of God with a hilarious "Ha! Ha! Ha!," but with a loving and grateful sob of the heart.

He who says, ". . . that my *joy* may be in you . . ." (John 15:11), also shares His *tears* with the family of Lazarus. In the final analysis, real tears and real joy go together.

A teardrop may *be* salty water. But, to me, a teardrop *means* a barrel-full of caring love.

"His Eye Is on the Sparrow"

Alongside my car, on the driveway in back of my home, I noticed a small object that seemed to move. Upon closer examination, I was shocked to find that it was a tiny baby bird. There it was on the cold, gray concrete. It had probably fallen from a nearby nest. Its head and legs looked so big compared to its tiny body. Soft gray feathers had just begun to sprout from its little wings.

I reached down and gently stroked its head. Its little mouth flew open as if expecting some food. Its eyes were still closed. Tenderly I picked up the little creature and placed it in my hand. I could feel the warmth of the little body in the palm of my hand. What a pathetic little thing it was.

But what was I supposed to do now? What does one do with a fledgling sparrow that has fallen from its nest? Frankly, I didn't have a clue. Someone suggested that I put it down on the patio where the other sparrows come to eat the bread crumbs I throw out there each day. So I tried this. Nothing happened. The other birds did not come to feed or care for the baby bird. After a while, I could see that ants were streaming in for the kill. I wasn't going to let that happen. I picked up the small bird and brushed off the hungry ants.

Next, I tried to feed the little creature myself. I mixed some powdered milk with water and tried to spoon-feed the tiny sparrow. Again, no success. It clamped its beak shut.

I could see that the little bird was getting weaker and weaker. I stroked its head. But no longer did the mouth open up. I was engulfed with feelings of hopelessness and helplessness. But I was determined that the sparrow would not die outside the house, alone in the cold.

I had to run upstairs to take care of something else for a short while. I left the bird in the kitchen briefly, but I quickly hurried back to it. Too late. It was lying on its side. I touched it.

No movement. It was dead. It was a sad moment for me. All alone in my kitchen it had died.

Suddenly I remembered something. The little sparrow had not died alone and unknown. God was there and He was aware. Jesus said, "Not one sparrow . . . . can fall to the ground without your Father knowing it" (Matthew 10:29, TLB). Wonderful! Praise the Lord. My baby bird did not die alone.

Jesus said even more than that, and it's worth repeating often. "So don't worry! You are more valuable to him than many sparrows" (Matthew 10:31 TLB).

When we fall out of the nest, the Father is there. When we fall to the ground under the pain and pressures of life, the Father is there. The tune of an old hymn fills my heart: "His eye is on the sparrow/and I know He watches me."

A SMILING JOGGER?

Have you ever seen a smiling jogger?

Probably never.

The typical jogger looks as though he just had a wisdom tooth pulled, or he just came away from a fight with his mother-in-law, or he is suffering from an abdominal attack. Grim-faced, obviously in agony, he stares straight ahead with every dismal step. When the intersection signal light turns red, he prances up and down on the corner, glancing at his watch or checking his pulse until the light turns green. Then he charges off again with great diligence, oblivious to man or beast.

Watch and see. The jogger never stops to pat a dog or chat with friends. At best, he'll manage a quick "hello" in passing. The sun may be shining, the birds may be singing lovely tunes, the flowers may be displaying myriad colors, the grass may be a fresh, beautiful green . . . but the serious-faced jogger is completely unaware of all this. If you shout a cheery "good morning," all you get in return is a limp wave of the hand. If that. But no smile, not even a trace. The typical jogger is totally preoccupied. He is therefore insensitive to everything and everyone else.

You know, it's possible to live just like that. We can plod along, unsmiling, preoccupied, and completely insensitive to people and things around us. But this is not the formula for a happy life. In fact, it is not *really* living at all.

Some time ago I read the story of a Catholic priest who discovered that he had terminal cancer. His doctors told him he had only six months to live at most. But instead of succumbing to feelings of despair and desperation, the priest wrote that he had never been happier. He said that this was by far the most enjoyable time of his life. He said he had become *really* alive to people and to nature for the first time.

For this priest, on the very brink of death, the roses had never smelled so sweet. The stars had never been so bright or majestic. The laughter of little children at play had never been such sweet music from heaven. Food had never tasted so good. Each new day was an exciting adventure. The Bible seemed so rich and relevant. The glow of the setting sun was a gift of God. The love of friends was so warm and so wonderful.

This priest, in the face of the inevitable end of his life, had become alive, *really* alive. He had come to know, as never before, what the psalmist meant when he exclaimed, "The heavens declare the glory of God; and the firmament sheweth his handiwork" (Psalm 19:1 KJV).

"This is the day which the Lord has made; let us rejoice and be glad in it" (Psalm 118:24).

FINDING HIDDEN TREASURE

Jesus was the Master picture painter. With colorful and vivid word pictures, He taught the multitudes and confided wisdom to His disciples. With a few well chosen words, Jesus was able to show the connection between the Kingdom of Heaven and the kingdom of earth. Take for example His story about the buried treasure: "The kingdom of heaven is like treasure hidden in a field, which a man found and covered up; then, in his joy, he goes and sells all that he has and buys that field" (Matthew 13:44).

Two thousand years later, we can still get the picture. A tenant farmer, with no joy and little reward in his work, laboriously plows a rocky and worn-out field. As he plods along, gripping the plow, he is probably thinking about his wife and children at home, living in a sorry little shack. The family has little food, even less money, few clothes, meager education, no luxuries, and, worst of all, precious little hope. Life is a grim existence and a bitter disappointment to this farmer and his loved ones.

But, hold on a minute! The poor farmer's plow strikes something in the dusty ground. Perhaps he curses the rocks as he stops to investigate. No, it's not a rock. It's a rusty old metal box with the lid now torn off by the plow. No doubt it's been buried here for years, decades, centuries, who knows? As he reaches down for the box, his heart is pounding with excitement. The glint of gold reflecting the sunlight catches his eye as he leans forward.

There it is! The old box is filled with treasure! The farmer feverishly brushes the dirt away from the box and feasts his eyes on the gold and jewels. Then, fighting to keep himself calm, he carefully covers the box with soil. Now full of energy, he sprints home. He gathers up everything he owns, sells it, and then he purchases the field immediately for above market price.

In one stroke, the poor man has more than he ever imagined possible. His family will never go hungry again. He has found an *earthly* treasure (literally) which has given him joy, happiness, security and hope where there had been none.

The purpose of Jesus' story is very clear. The ultimate treasure in life is to find the kingdom of God. The kingdom of God is *the* treasure that provides the *ultimate* rewards of life. It is a treasure that provides ". . . joy unspeakable and full of glory" (1 Peter 1:8 KJV). It is a treasure which gives ". . . the peace of God, which passeth all understanding" (Philippians 4:7 KJV). It is a treasure which offers forgiveness of sin and life everlasting. It is a treasure that brings with it Jesus' promise, "I am come that they might have life and that they might have it more abundantly" (John 10:10 KJV).

It is a treasure which is real and ready to be found.

We do not have to plod along in "silent desperation."

Life, meaning, and happiness begin when we can say, "Eureka! I have found it!"

STORMIE JONES

I just read a touching story about a six-year-old girl that made me realize again how wonderful love is and how much we all need more of it.

Little Stormie Jones, from the town of Cumby, Texas, had to undergo a liver and heart transplant operation which lasted sixteen hours. This was the first time a simultaneous heart and liver transplant had ever been attempted by surgeons anywhere in the world. The medical staff at Children's Hospital in Pittsburgh anxiously waited and watched. When little Stormie first regained consciousness after the operation, she warmly greeted her mother with those three beautiful words: "I love you."

She had a borrowed heart, but it was full of love for her mother.

Someone gave me a memorable paragraph entitled "The Mystery of Love":

> Love makes you feel special. It changes everyone for the better. It is one commodity that multiplies when you give it away. The more you spread it around, the more you are able to hang onto it, because it keeps coming back to you. Where love is concerned, it pays to be an absolute spendthrift. It cannot be bought nor sold, so give it away! Throw it away. Splash it all over! Empty your pockets! Shake the basket! Turn it upside down! Shower it on everyone—even those who don't deserve it! You may startle them into behaving in a way you never dreamed possible. Not only is it the sweet mystery of life, it is the most powerful motivator known to humankind.

When I read about Stormie Jones' childlike expression of love, I thought about the time my seven-year-old granddaughter, Shannon, looked at me with a quizzical expression and assured me of her love by saying, "Papa, I love you more than any other fat man."

In my best moments, I not only desire to receive more love from others, I also want to love others more. But I have to admit that I find some people *so* difficult to love. Perhaps if I were more childlike, I would be able to love people more.

Even myself.

"There Is No Better Time"

While vacationing on the coast of Washington one recent summer, I went to a doctor in a small town for an infection on the back of my neck. The doctor looked at the problem, gave me an evaluation, and then wrote up a prescription. Finally, pointing his finger at my well-rounded midsection, he quietly but firmly remarked, "That is more of a problem than your neck. You need to lose about forty pounds."

I responded with a defensive grin and the normal statement for a fat and hungry vacationer, "Yeah, I know you're right, and I plan to take if off as soon as I get back home. That will be a much better time."

This thirty-seven-year-old physician from New York University folded his arms across his chest and said, profoundly, "There is no better time."

We can all take it from there. You and I know it well: there is a terrible urge in all of us to feel that the future is a better time to do the difficult things we know we ought to be doing today. It is always convenient and comforting to think that there is a better time coming up. Probably very soon, too. But, not today.

How many times have we all tried pushing today's tough decisions into vague tomorrows?

"I am going to lose weight right after my vacation."

"I am going to quit smoking right after my birthday."

"I am going to quit drinking after New Years."

"I am planning to start a daily devotional time very soon."

"One of these days, I am going to become a Christian."

"I am going to get right with God."

"I am going to start reading the Bible every day."

Et cetera. Et cetera.

Out there, someday, somehow, somewhere, I am going to do what I know God wants me to do right now.

In our hearts, we all know that this "country doctor" was right on target when he said, *"There is no better time."*

For the truth is, nobody ever *actually* started a diet, or quit smoking, or turned over a new leaf, *tomorrow.* Think about it! Today is always the only possible "day of decision."

The Bible affirms it: "Now is the accepted time; behold, now is the day of salvation" (2 Corinthians 6:2 KJV).

"This is the day which the Lord has made; let us rejoice and be glad in it" (Psalm 118:24).

Our relationship with God must be in the "todays." Not the "tomorrows."

"There is *no better time."*

Dear You

LIFE IS A ONE-WAY TRIP

I am fascinated by the guidance systems that God has built into His creation. I want to give you another amazing example of God's guidance, the story of the Monarch butterfly.

Monarch butterflies are tiny, fragile members of God's creation which weigh little more than small feathers. Nonetheless, they manage to fly thousands of miles to spend the winter in the warmer climates of California. Each year these flocks of small butterflies move from the East Coast to the West Coast. Each year they come in October and arrive in Pacific Grove, California. Here, an estimated two million Monarchs spend the winter, year after year, on the same trees within a six-acre area.

Think of it! These minute creatures find the very same trees each year. And—this part is astounding to me—since their life span is so short, they can make the round trip only one time. How then, without leader or guide or guideposts, do these midget wayfarers find their way to this small six-acre plot? Remember, not one of them ever took the trip before. Every one of them is a "rookie."

There is only one answer: God provided a guidance system for them.

Come to think of it, we're all in the same sort of navigational quandary. Life is a one-way journey. None of us has ever made this trip before.

We are all just a bunch of amateur travelers in this life. We're all rookie ballplayers, so to speak. We are amateurs at living and amateurs at dying—and amateurs at finding our way all along the path. Therefore, we all need to tune in, like the Monarch butterfly, to the Guide of all Creation. The Bible says that we can: "Trust in the Lord with all thine heart; and lean not unto thine own understanding. In all thy ways acknowledge him, and *he shall direct thy paths*" (Proverbs 3:5, 6 KJV).

Believe it!

ON FOOLS AND PILGRIMS

The assumption that material possessions will bring satisfaction and happiness is hard to shake.

A few years ago, I was talking to a man who had been a professor of New Testament studies for over thirty years. I asked him, "When are you going to retire?" He replied, "As soon as I get to be sixty-five. I can't wait." I asked, "What are you going to do when you retire?" To my surprise, he said, "I am going to buy more property."

As I conversed with the professor, it became clear that he was very impatient with his life's "calling," that is, to study and share the New Testament. He was even dissatisfied with his comfortable lifestyle and pending secure retirement. He was "chafing at the bit" to try to make a fortune in real estate before he died. I was astonished. I still haven't gotten over it. Didn't this Christian man, expert in the teaching of the New Testament, know that "A man's life does not consist in the abundance of his possessions" (Luke 12:15)?

The idea that material possessions will bring satisfaction is hard to get rid of, even for Christians.

In fact, Jesus called a rich farmer a "fool" because he subscribed to this idea (Luke 12:20). This farmer was honest, industrious, and successful. His crops were consistently bountiful to the point that he needed bigger barns to hold the harvest. In the eyes of the world, and in his own eyes, this man was a "winner." He had it made. But Jesus, contradicting all "appearances," called him a fool. Why?

Jesus called him a fool because he didn't keep *things* at their proper distance and in their proper perspective. He said to his possessions, "You are my life." He failed to make the distinction between *him* and *his*. His life was lost in his livelihood. He was not concerned with the inner life but only with the outer, material life. "*Things* are a jealous god; they brook no rival."

Jesus called this farmer a fool because he was terribly self-centered. He speaks constantly of "I," "my," and "mine." The man cannot see beyond himself.

Jesus said he was a fool also because he failed to recognize how much God, and God-given nature, was involved in his success: the sap from the trees, the fertility of the soil, the sunshine, the rain, the returning seasons of the year, and the growth potential built into the seeds.

Jesus called him a fool because he was bereft of feeling for others. He had no consciousness of the fact that others did the plowing for him, others built the barns, others gathered the crops. The farmer did not accumulate his wealth all alone. But he took all the credit anyway. And all he was concerned with was his own ease, his own drinks, his own merry-making.

Jesus called him a fool because he was completely unaware of the temporality of life. He made his priorities accordingly. He should have recognized that he was not a permanent resident, just a *pilgrim.*

We are all "pilgrims" who are called to be "rich toward God."

THE HIGHWIRE WALK OF LIFE

I watched the TV screen in horror. Right before my eyes, a famous company of acrobats formed a human pyramid on a high-wire. There was an unexpected, ominous wobble, and then the acrobats all tumbled and fell squirming to the hard ground below. Spectators screamed and shrieked in disbelief as attendants rushed to the aid of the fallen acrobats. On the circus floor, before the incredulous gaze of all the spectators, lay dead and injured bodies.

The "Flying Wallendas," a family of acrobats who had been a featured act in circuses around the world for many years, had finally and fatally fallen. They had performed their difficult feats flawlessly so many times, and they were so assured of their ability and precision, that they had long ago removed all safety nets below the high-wire.

It was a fatal decision.

It is always a fatal decision when we assume that nothing harmful can happen. In fact, it scares me to think how easy it is to get that idea. That's when I need to remember the words of the apostle Paul, "Let him who thinks he stands take heed lest he fall" (1 Corinthians 10:12). And the fall can be fatal.

It is so terribly easy to be smug and self-assured. We can easily be lulled into being so comfortable and secure about our health, our family, our finances, our positions, et cetera, that we can walk the high-wires of life unaware that there might be cancer cells building in our bodies, or that our closest relationship might actually be crumbling, or that our economic security is on the verge of collapse, or that our reputation and popularity are waning. Even worse, we may be abysmally unaware—as were the "Flying Wallendas"—that life itself is almost over.

"Let him who thinks he stands take heed lest he fall" (1 Corinthians 10:12).

The walk of life is a tricky business. It is a high-wire act all the way. Of course, God does not want us to walk in fear and anxiety, but He does want us to walk in humility and gratitude. He does want us to be always aware of our humanity and temporality. He does want us to remember that we are here as His guests in His universe. Therefore, as the Bible says—
"We walk by faith" (2 Corinthians 5:7).

"The Lord Is My Shepherd"

Dr. J. Wilbur Chapman was traveling through the Highlands of Scotland when he met a young boy tending his sheep. Always ready to witness for the Lord, Dr. Chapman asked the boy, "Do you know how to recite the Twenty-third Psalm?" The timid little boy admitted that he did not, so Chapman taught him the first five words of the Psalm, "The Lord is my shepherd." To help the boy remember these wonderful words, Chapman had the boy hold up his hand, and he assigned one word to each finger, beginning with the thumb: "The—Lord—is—my—shepherd."

Months later, Dr. Chapman was in the same area of the Highlands again, so he decided to stop by and visit the shepherd boy. Not finding him out in the hills with the sheep, Chapman inquired at a nearby hut, where he found the lad's mother. She had tragic news. While out tending the sheep, the boy had been caught in a terrible blizzard and lost his life. Tearfully, she told Chapman about the way the young boy had treasured the five words of the Twenty-third Psalm, especially the way he had held his fourth finger and repeated the word, *"my."* He would often say these words of comfort, and, holding onto his fourth finger, he would emphasize, "*My* shepherd, *My* shepherd." She continued, "When they found his body in the deep snow, his two hands were sticking out. He was clasping his fourth finger! We *knew* what that meant."

In a world of certain blizzards, we must have *personal* relationships with our Shepherd-Lord. Jesus Christ is indeed the Good Shepherd, but, unless He is "my" shepherd, it does me no good whatsoever. I cannot face the blizzards of life unless He is *my* shepherd. I need a personal shepherd for my personal blizzards. I must be able to say, "I know whom I have believed" (2 Timothy 1:12). And I had better be prepared at all times.

"The Lord is *my* shepherd" (Psalm 23:1).

JONI'S JOY

Have you had some rotten luck? Are you bitter about it? That's the normal, "human" reaction.

But listen to the amazing story of Joni Eareckson Tada. She was a beautiful, active, seventeen-year-old American girl, filled with life and optimism. One day she dove into Chesapeake Bay, and it proved to be a tragic, yet triumphant, turning point in her young life.

The water was too shallow where Joni dove. She broke her neck, and despite the best efforts of her doctors, she was permanently paralyzed from the shoulders down. For many years she has been confined to a wheel chair, unable to move either her arms or her legs. Bitter about it? At first, yes.

But you should see her now. She is the picture of radiance and happiness. All bitterness is gone.

Although it takes Joni three hours each morning to get ready for the day, she faces life with a beautiful smile. She gives her testimony in words that glow and flow with warm Christian love.

Joni is also a gifted painter. One of her paintings hangs in the White House in Washington, D.C. Holding the paint brush between her teeth, Joni has turned out many acclaimed paintings and Christmas card drawings. Despite her enormous handicap, she travels all over the United States giving her testimony for Christ and presenting her remarkable works of art.

What does Joni say to those who come to meet her and to see her art? Are you ready for this? She says that she is thankful to God for what happened because it opened a door of ministry for Christ.

No wonder thousands of people have brushed aside tears of sympathy and of thanksgiving when they have heard her radiant witness. I join them.

I also say, Lord, forgive me for my lack of thankfulness. Here I am with two good legs and two good arms. I take them for granted. I take so very, very much for granted all the time. Then, when I see Joni's tremendous thankfulness, and when I see the thankfulness of the apostle Paul in spite of his great sufferings for Christ, then I wonder if I am really on the right wavelength.

Thank you, Joni. You have made me thankful. Thank you for giving a living demonstration of the—

"Attitude of Gratitude."

Dear You

Winning the Race

All of us are in the race of our life!

In his day the apostle Paul was fully aware of all the excitement of the Olympic Games. He says, "To win a contest you must deny yourself many things that would keep you from doing your best. An athlete goes to all this trouble just to win a blue ribbon or a silver cup, but we do it for a heavenly reward that never disappears. So I run straight to the goal with purpose in every step . . ." (1 Corinthians 9:25, 26 TLB).

All of us are in a race against time. Time is an untiring competitor. Like "ol' man river," it "just keeps rolling along." Things I thought had happened two years ago turn out to have been five or six years ago. Time is outrunning me. To win, we must "redeem the time" (Ephesians 5:16), and fill it with thoughts of God and of continued service to Him.

All of us are in a race against sin. The Bible says, ". . . let us strip off anything that slows us down or holds us back, and especially those *sins* that wrap themselves so tightly around our feet and trip us up" (Hebrews 12:1 TLB). To win, we must have God's continuous forgiveness and power.

All of us are in a race against "this world." It is ever so easy to "let the world press us into its mold." All of us are competing against the constant subtle pressure of a sinful and secular world which caters to the self and to the sensuous. To win, we must be in the best spiritual condition possible. This involves a disciplined "mindset": that we will "pray without ceasing" and we will "set our affection on things above, not on things on the earth" (Colossians 3:2 KJV).

All of us are in a race against spiritual lethargy. Ministers are not exempt. Even ministers are supposed to grow spiritually. We are *all* either growing or shrinking all the time. It is all *too* easy to get out of spiritual "shape." The apostle Paul feared this and said so: "I fear that after enlisting others for the race,

I myself might be declared unfit and ordered to stand aside" (1 Corinthians 9:27 TLB).

I often hear people speak of their spiritual lives in the past tense. "I used to pray every day." "I used to go to church." "I used to teach a class at church." "I used to sing in the choir." "I used to read my Bible every day." And so on and so forth . . . .

To win, we must confess our coldness and pray for heat . . . . We've got enough light! God is able to restore *the joy of our salvation.*"

God has put each of us in this race and He is able to make every one of us a *winner!*

THE PARABLE IN THE PARKING TICKET

As I was nearing home after my morning walk, I noticed that a parking ticked was perched on the windshield of a car parked down the street from my house. *Poor guy,* I thought, *that's twenty-eight bucks out of his pocket.* Then it occurred to me that it was then Tuesday between 7:30 A.M. and 9:30 A.M. Parking is prohibited along this street during those two hours each week so that the large city street-sweeper can swoop through and clean the street.

Uh-oh, I thought, *did I forget, too? Did I leave my car on the street?* I quickened my pace. I peered ahead. Yes, my car *is* on the street. And there is that blasted yellow citation envelope on my front windshield! Doggone it, they got me—again!

Don't the police have anything better to do? Are there no more criminals to catch? Can't a citizen park his own car in front of his own house without being harassed?

I was fuming. I yanked the envelope off the windshield, tempted to tear it up. In fact, several years ago, I had done just that, but I learned the hard way the folly of that reaction. (When I went to pay my annual vehicle registration fee, I had to also pay double fines for the two citations I had angrily torn up.) So, I was not in a pleasant mood as I strode into my house with my $28 parking ticket firmly in hand.

Still trying to calm myself down and to put this irritating event into better "perspective," I mentally reviewed the reasons for the parking regulation I had violated (and which was clearly posted on signs along the street). When I first moved here some years ago, my neighbors were angry because city officials had allowed this street to become very dirty. The residents wrote letters, circulated petitions, made phone calls, held meetings, lobbied, and agitated. They demanded that the city do something about it.

They got action. The city starting cleaning the street every Tuesday morning between seven-thirty and nine-thirty. It was also, of course, made illegal to park on the street during the cleaning time. Signs to that effect were posted.

I began to realize that the law which had "bitten" me was not bad, but good. If I wanted a clean street in front of my house, then I had to get my car off the street when the sweeper came to do its job. The law was for *my* good. It was certainly no fault of the law that I kept forgetting to do my part.

This is true in life. How many times we rail against the laws of God. We often feel that His laws cramp our style, deny us pleasure, block our freedom. It is more than just humor when we say, "Everything fun is either immoral, illegal, or fattening."

But, in truth, we know that God's laws are for our own good. They are written into the very fiber of our beings. They are there because God loves us.

When we sin, we don't really sin against law, we sin against love. God wants us to be happy. Happiness and holiness go together. You can't have one without the other. The psalmist says of the happy man, "His delight is in the *law* of the Lord, and in his *law* he meditates day and night" (Psalm 1:2).

"Open my eyes, that I may behold wondrous things out of thy *law*" (Psalm 119:18).

HE IS LISTENING!

Many years ago in Mountain View, California, something awakened me in the middle of the night. At first I didn't know what it was. I sat up and listened in the darkness. Then I heard it again. It sounded like a little child crying on the front porch of the house. It couldn't be that, I thought. About then, my wife, Vivian, sensing something also, awakened and said, "What is it?" I said, "Listen. I thought I heard a child crying on the front porch." Then we both heard it again, the unmistakable sob of a little child.

I sprang out of bed and opened the front door. There, in the doorway, clad in a white nightgown, stood a tiny little blonde child, her large blue eyes filled with tears. What a pathetic sight she was. I picked her up in my arms and held her close to me. She snuggled into my neck. Her sobbing subsided and her fears seemed to diminish.

But I didn't get to hold her for long. Her mother, who was out looking for her lost child, saw the light coming from our open front door. She came quickly and took the child into her own arms. The mother explained that her own front door had been left open and the little girl had wandered out into the summer night by herself.

I've thought about that incident many times since. A sudden cry for help in the darkness of the night. Thank God, I heard the cry and responded.

But I wonder how many other times there have been cries of distress in the darkness of night, and I was too deeply asleep or too self-centered to hear and respond. How often we all are so preoccupied that we do not hear the cries of distress coming from others as they wander around in the darkness seeking help.

Jesus is always listening for the cry of distress. Even in the din of the crowd, He heard the voice of blind Bartimaeus calling out for healing (Mark 10:46–52). Jesus heard the cries of the lepers and He responded to their distress (Luke 17:12–14).

Are you going through a period of darkness in your life? Are you wandering around in distress? Then cry out to Him. He knows your voice as a mother knows the voices, and the cries, of every one of her children.

When we are going through the darkness of night, we can cry out with faith for we know one thing for certain.

He is listening!

A Lesson in Contentment

We were all thrilled as we rode along in the borrowed 1973 motorhome on our way to San Francisco. My son, Don, and I were in the front two seats. Don's wife, Shirley, would bring us cold drinks from the built-in refrigerator. A nice little toilet compartment was also available for our use. As we drove along, we could hear Shirley and her mother-in-law laughing as they played a game of dominoes on the built-in table in the rear of the vehicle.

Boy, what fun it was. I was so glad to know that the motorhome could be purchased for as little as five thousand dollars. What a bargain for such a fine old motorhome with so much equipment, all of it working. What fun we could have with this vehicle. *Why, we'll take a trip in it up to Seattle next summer.* "Why stop there?" someone else chimed in. "Let's go all the way up to Alaska! Why not?"

We were completely carried away with how nice the motorhome looked, how well it ran, how comfortable and convenient it was, and how many wonderful features it had. There had never been so much motorhome for so little price. We just *had* to buy it.

Happy as we could be, we stopped for breakfast in Paso Robles. As we left the restaurant, we noticed that there was a motorhome sales lot right alongside our parked vehicle. Shirley spotted a nice, clean-looking 1979 motorhome of the same make as "ours." It was on "special" and open for inspection. We all just had to take a peek.

This motorhome was roomier inside than the one we were driving. It had a big, beautiful shower and toilet compartment across the back. It had a shiny stove, wide windows, a new refrigerator, two comfy little couches facing each other. And everything was polished to a sparkle, a real "showcase." And to think, it was on "sale" for only $12,800. Like the advertising jingle says, "Who could ask for anything more?"

When we got back to "our" motorhome, it was the ugliest thing on the road. How dirty and dingy it looked! How gloomy it was inside. How cramped. How drab and old it seemed. And when we got going again, how rough it seemed to ride!

We muttered our way along the highway for awhile, and then we all broke into loud laughter. We suddenly realized how, in one short hour, we had gone from delight to depression, from satisfaction to dissatisfaction, from an "attitude of gratitude" to an attitude of envy.

How true to life. How often we fail to be truly happy because instead of being satisfied with what we have, we are constantly looking for something newer and better on the horizon. We are looking for a better wife or better husband, a better job, a better church, a better son or daughter, better vehicles, a better house, better health, et cetera. If only our "situation" was better, we could then be happy persons. But it never seems to get enough better.

Turn the dial of your heart and beam in on the message of the apostle Paul: "I have learned, in whatever state I am, to be content" (Philippians 4:11).

WHAT SHALL I DO FIRST?

Every morning I have the same struggle. Shall I go down the stairs, open the front door, pick up the *Los Angeles Times*, climb back up the stairs and read all the news (most of it bad)? Or shall I stay upstairs, open the Bible and read the news (all of it good)? Ever have a struggle like that?

Now, you would think that after all these years of being a Christian and a pastor, I would have won the struggle long ago. But I haven't. It's crazy and ridiculous, but true. Early in the morning I hear the sound when the paper lands on the sidewalk in front of my house. There it is, outside on the ground, full of news about what's going on in the world, full of stories about sports, full of graphic pictures, and on top of everything else there is always "Peanuts."

After all, I don't want to get legalistic. The *whole* day belongs to God, doesn't it? What difference does it make what I read *first*? What am I becoming, anyway? Some kind of a nut? A fanatic?

There is something profoundly simple, necessary, and rewarding in starting the day with God, the Bible, and prayer. It is a recognition that the spiritual has priority over the secular. There is a nice, comfy, at-home feeling when we "seek *first* his kingdom and his righteousness" (Matthew 6:33).

Then we have a sense that we are starting the day "right" that God has given to us. Then we become aware of the timeless as well as the temporary, of the unseen as well as the seen. It is a time of new spiritual discoveries.

Dr. Dale Moody, the well known theologian from Southern Seminary, was a living demonstration of this principle when he spoke at the "John Bailey Lectures." Moody told us that all his life he had made a practice of starting the day with Bible study and prayer. At the beginning of his lecture each day, he would share with us a new discovery he had made that very morning

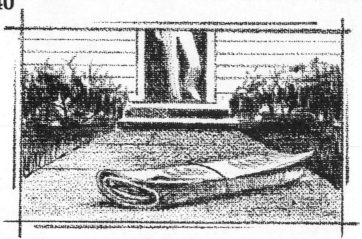

in his "quiet time." His voice was always full of emotion and excitement and he would conclude, "I never saw that before!"

Lord, forgive us for the many times we have failed to put You first and have instead gone our own way in our human wisdom and human energy. Help us this day to spend time with You before we spend time with anyone else. Help us to listen to You before we listen to anyone else.

And thank You, Lord, that I am still troubled about the struggle.

THE LOVE OF MONEY

Not long ago, I had the miserable and uncomfortable feel ing of watching the members of a family scheming and fighting to grab the money and property of another family member who had just died. I could not help but remember the words, "The love of money is the root of all evil," (1 Timothy 6:10). Also, these words of Jesus, "A man's life consists not in the abundance of the things he possesses" (Luke 12:15).

In 1923, a group of the world's most successful financiers and business tycoons met at the Edgewater Beach Hotel in Chicago. These men controlled more wealth than there was in the United States Treasury at that time. They were all heralded by the press for their notable successes. The youth of the nation were urged to follow their examples. But it is astonishing to note what happened to these mighty men during the next twenty-five years, during which the Great Depression struck.

Charles Schwab, president of the country's largest independent steel company, died a bankrupt man and lived on borrowed money for the last five years of his life.

Samuel Insull, president of the greatest utility company in the country, died a fugitive from justice and penniless in a foreign land.

Arthur Cotten, the greatest wheat speculator of them all, died abroad, totally insolvent.

Richard Whitney, president of the New York Stock Exchange, was sent to Sing Sing penitentiary for his crooked dealings.

Albert Fall, a one-time member of the Cabinet of the President of the United States, was pardoned from prison at the end of his life so he could die at home.

Jesse Livermore, the greatest "bear" on Wall Street, committed suicide, all alone.

Leon Frazer, president of the Bank of International Settlements, also committed suicide.

Ivar Krueger, head of the greatest "monopoly" of the day, took his own life as well.

The Pacific Institute, which printed this story, concluded by saying, "All these men learned well the art of making money, but not one of them learned how to live."

In contrast, I'm sure we could all make a list of fine Christian men and women of wealth who have learned not only the art of making money, but also the art of living for Christ. But this unusual combination is not easy to achieve. There is a greedy streak in all of us. Even in preachers, I'm afraid. Jesus is very clear about the relationship of God and gold: "You cannot serve two masters: God and money. For you will hate one and love the other, or else the other way around" (Matthew 6:24 TLB).

How we all need to humbly pray, "Lord, help me to set my affections on things above and not on things of the earth."

"For where your treasure is, there will your heart be also" (Matthew 6:21).

THE ANXIETY ATTACK

Last night I awoke about three A.M. Couldn't sleep.

My mind was mulling over all the problems of the church, all the problems the people were facing in their personal lives, all the things I should have done already and all the things I still needed to do, all the annoying little things that people do and say. All, all, all . . . .

No use. No sleep. I rolled from one side to the other. Finally, as dawn approached, I dozed off for about an hour.

As I was driving to church, my mind was still at it, thrashing away frenetically. I gripped the steering wheel tensely. My chest felt tight. My body was taut. I was physically in the car, and I was even managing to drive somehow, but my mind was worrying all over the place. Here it was, a lovely, sunny day, and I was trying to be a modern Atlas. I was carrying the cares of the world on my shoulders. I was just a weary, wooden worrier.

Then a thought hit me. Hey! What are you trying to do? Run the universe? After all, you didn't create it. And God didn't assign you the task. So, stop trying to play God. Do you think that God has no stake in the universe or in your own life? Do you think God is unaware of all these problems? After all, God has seen problems and people come and go. But the sun still rises in the East and sets in the West, and life still goes on . . . with new problems and new people.

As I drove along, the bigger my thoughts about God were, the smaller my problems became. By this time, I was driving with one hand, leaning back in the seat, and starting to enjoy the beauty of the scenery and the sunshine.

So many times we miss so much, when we trust only in mind and muscle. Tell me the truth: Are you enjoying today? Or are you so wrapped up in self-pity, worry, and feverish activity that you cannot smell a rose, feel the sunshine, see the stars, or hear the laughter of little children?

Stop it. Remember that God has a stake in your life. He wants you to relax and enjoy this day. And when you go to bed tonight, say a little prayer, put your head down on the pillow, and go to sleep. And—don't worry.

God will take care of the universe while you are asleep. He has been doing it for a long, long, *long* time.

"ABIDE WITH ME"

Millions of people around the world have been singing this song for over one hundred years. It has blessed, comforted, and given spiritual strength to carry on in the face of suffering, loneliness, and emptiness. If ever there were truly "a sermon in song," this is it.

The hymn was written by a preacher. Henry Francis Lyte, the minister of a church in Devonshire, England for twenty years, wrote the lyrics in 1847. When his health began to fail, Lyte made plans to spend the next winter in the warmer climate of Italy. But it was not to be. He became too weak to make that arduous trip. But not too weak to preach.

One Sunday, against the wishes of his closest friends, who feared for his well-being, Lyte preached his farewell sermon to his much-beloved and much-loving people. After the service, in great weakness, he made his way home to the church parsonage. There he wrote the lines of this immortal hymn, "Abide with Me."

Although he was only fifty-four years of age, he knew that the shadows of death were quickly falling. He died shortly afterward. His last words were, "Peace, joy!"

These words, written by a man who knew he was about to die, are indeed a sermon in song!

> Abide with me; fast falls the eventide;
> The darkness deepens; Lord, with me abide!
> When other helpers fail, and comforts flee,
> Help of the helpless, O abide with me.
>
> Swift to its close ebbs out life's little day,
> Earth's joys grow dim, its glories pass away;
> Change and decay in all around I see,
> O Thou, who changest not, abide with me.

What perception and discovery. The world we live in is constantly changing and constantly decaying. Even these bodies of ours are changing, passing things. But Lyte had discovered that there is an abiding Reality in a world of change and decay. That is Jesus Christ. "O Thou, who changest not, abide with me."

Henry Francis Lyte had discovered what the writer of the Book of Hebrews discovered, "Jesus Christ is the same yesterday and today and for ever" (Hebrews 13:8).

We all need to discover, and to re-discover, that Jesus Christ is the only unchanging reality in a world of change. It is so easy to get attached to what is changing. It is so easy to "take the fake." The lure of the temporal is very attractive and extremely compelling. Listen to Jesus, "If you abide in me, and my words abide in you, ask whatever you will, and it shall be done for you" (John 15:7).

Lyte's closing words say it all—

"In life, in death, O Lord, abide with me."

RESTORATION

Restoration! What a wonderful word it is! What a wonderful idea it is! What a wonderful experience it is! Restoration is exactly the opposite of being thrown out or discarded.

I still remember one time when I was a teenage boy. I pulled some foolish stunt, and I was afraid to go home and face the wrath of my stern Scottish father. For several days I stayed with friends. But I longed to go back home. Finally, through the grapevine, I got word that I would be welcome at home. My dad was not the type to give me a hero's welcome, but it felt so good just to be restored as a son and as a member of the family.

The apostle Peter experienced the joy of restoration. When the heat was on, after Jesus had been captured, Peter denied his relationship to his Lord three times. But when the risen Christ served breakfast on the shore of the Sea of Galilee, He gave Peter the chance, three times, to affirm his love for his Lord. Three times Jesus restored him to a place of service, saying to Peter: "Feed my sheep" (John 21:15–17).

And what a restoration project Peter was. From being wishy-washy and undependable, Peter became indeed a "rock." He became a fearless conduit of God's love and His restoration power. According to tradition, when Peter was condemned to death, he asked to be crucified upside-down because he said he was not worthy to be crucified in the same way his Lord had been.

To see a person restored is a beautiful sight. A friend of mine told me this story. He and another deacon in a church in a small midwest town were walking down the main street on a Saturday night when they spotted one of their other deacons sprawled on the curbstone. They found that the man was miserably drunk, disgracing himself in public. But they didn't give up on him or condemn him or ignore him.

The two deacons picked up the drunken man and walked him around the back streets for hours. Then they took him home, filled him with coffee, gave him a shower, and lovingly tended to him till he sobered up. The man wept in shame and asked for forgiveness. They prayed with him, gave him a clean shirt, and brushed off his suit. The next morning *that* man served communion with the other deacons in church. That is restoration.

All of us "have sinned and fall short . . ." (Romans 3:23). All of us have stumbled. All of us, in one way or another, have denied our Lord. All of us have gone through the agony of ruptured relations with God. All of us have felt that we have "blown it."

But isn't it wonderful to know that—since day one—God has one loving project in mind for all of us.

Restoration!

"More"

Not all "four letter words" are nasty words.

Take, for example, the word "more." It can be used to signify *quality* or *quantity*. Or it can mean both quality and quantity wrapped up together. The hymn-writer wraps them up together in his heart-felt plea to the Lord:

> *More* love to Thee, O Christ, *more* love to Thee.
> Hear Thou the prayer I make, on bended knee.
> This is my earnest plea, *more* love, O Christ, to Thee.
> *More* love to Thee.

The hymn-writer's plea clearly includes both the quality and the quantity of love. He cries for a deeper love and for *more* of the same.

Jesus assures us that if God's concerns include the falling of a little sparrow and keeping track of the number of hairs on our heads, then we have nothing to fear, because He has *more* concern for us. He says, "Fear not, therefore; you are of *more* value than many sparrows" (Matthew 10:31).

Jesus also assures us that if human fathers will, and do, respond to their children's requests for food, it is certain that our Heavenly Father will do even *more*. Jesus draws this conclusion: "If you then, who are evil, know how to give good gifts to your children, how much *more* shall the heavenly Father give the Holy Spirit to those who ask him" (Luke 11:13)?

Jesus assures us that as the Good Shepherd, He has come to lead us into spiritual pastures which will give us meaning and purpose in life. We will cease to be sheep wandering in the wilderness. "I am come that they might have life, and that they might have it *more* abundantly" (John 10:10 KJV). Not just an abundant life, but a *more* abundant life!

The apostle Paul was a man who knew all about this kind of life. He knew full well that, "If any one is in Christ, he is a new creation" (2 Corinthians 5:17). It had changed him from being a prosecutor to being a proclaimer of the Christian faith. He was the personification of this truth. Above all, he was certain that the love of God, as manifested in Jesus Christ, was able to carry us through all the tribulations, distresses, and perils that life can possibly hit us with.

The apostle could look all these difficulties in the face and say, "In all these things we are *more* than conquerors through him who loved us" (Romans 8:37). Note, we are *more* than conquerors.

No, not all four letter words are nasty words.

Wherever we are spiritually, in quantity and quality, we are able to have—

MORE.

THE ALTERNATE ROAD

There, in front of us, were the bright red brake lights of thousands of cars clogging the I-5 freeway into Los Angeles. Our schedule called for us to get Bonnie and Heather, two of my granddaughters, to the train station in downtown L.A. before 8:40 P.M., when the last train was departing for Del Mar. The two girls had to report to work early the next morning. But there was now only forty-five minutes before that train pulled out of grand old Union Station and headed south.

Gloom began to fill our motorhome as we crept along, barely moving. The homeward-bound holiday weekend traffic was turning the highway into a gigantic parking lot. We had made good progress all the way from San Francisco. But now this!

My son, Don, was driving the motorhome. His tired eyes showed his concern for his two lovely daughters as we inched along, lurching forward a few yards or so, then coming to yet another complete halt. We repeatedly glanced at our watches. As the minutes ticked away, we realized that we were on a "failure trip." We would never make it in time.

Then an idea came to me. We would soon be coming to a different freeway, the 210, or "Foothill," freeway. It did not lead directly into central L.A. but to Pasadena. I thought, *Why not leave this crowded mess and drive quickly to Pasadena on this other freeway which won't be crowded, then take the Pasadena freeway into Los Angeles?* This would be a longer route but with lighter traffic all the way, a sort of "back door" route to Union Station.

I mentioned the idea to Don. He said, "Dad, you might have something there. I think it might work. It's a cinch we're dead going this way." We all agreed there was really no alternative but to try this desperate "end-run."

Don drove off the clogged I-5, and we were soon speeding along toward Pasadena on an almost empty freeway. The

Pasadena freeway into L.A. was just as deserted. We got encouraged again, and finally excited, as we raced along toward Union Station. We actually arrived a few minutes ahead of time. We hustled the girls to the gate, and they were soon happily on their way home.

An alternate road made the difference. An alternate route made the failure trip into a victory trip.

How many people today are on a crowded road, frustrated by slow progress, on a trip which is certain to end in failure. It is a road of disillusionment, frustration, and disappointment, all shared by the masses of *this world*.

But wait! There is an alternate road! A spiritual road! Jesus says, "I am the way . . . the truth, and the life" (John 14:6). It is all too easy to get clogged up on the sinful, sensual, and secular road, the road of "this world." Jesus says to all of us, "Get off that road." He says, "I am the alternate route. I will get you to the spiritual station."

ON TIME.

TOUGH LOVE

A few years ago I was introduced to the term, "tough love." The more I have reflected on the meaning of this term, the more I have been captured by its truth and its relevance to life in our world today.

"Tough love" means that you are willing to allow, even to encourage, someone you love to make hard decisions, to endure hard work, and to live with suffering for their own good, even though it hurts, really hurts, to stand by and watch it happen. It is always hard to override feelings of sympathy and to silently watch someone we love go through pain and emotional hardships. In fact, it takes "tough love."

"Soft love," on the other hand, is where we rush in to help the one we love to *avoid* tough decisions, and to avoid hard work and the suffering they actually need for their own growth and development. Overprotection in the name of love is "overkill" in its worst form.

I shall ever be grateful to my Dad for allowing me to sell newspapers at six o'clock in the mornings at the end of the streetcar line in Hawthorne, California, when I was a little boy, starting at only six years of age. I'm sure that Dad was fully aware of me standing out there on winter mornings in the chilly and sometimes rainy weather. But he never tried to coax me back to the warm house. He had "tough love."

That's where the apostle Peter made his mistake. He was guilty of "soft love." He tried to spare Jesus the suffering and pain of the cross. For that, he received a stern reply from Jesus, "Out of my sight, Satan! You are a stumbling block to me; you do not have in mind the things of God, but the things of men" (Matthew 16:23 NIV).

I like what William Barclay says about "tough love":

The hardest temptation of all is the temptation which comes from protecting love. There are times when fond love seeks to deflect us from the perils of the path of God; but real love (tough love) is not the love which holds the knight at home when he should go out to battle, but the love which sends him out to obey the commandment of chivalry which is given, not to make life easy, but to make life great.

It is "tough love," not "soft love," which people need to make them great.

Lord, make us tough enough to give "tough love" to those we love.

THE JUMPER CABLE

The other day, I got into my car and turned the ignition key to start the engine. Nothing happened.

Uh-oh, I thought, *what's the matter here?* I pushed the horn. No sound. I reached to pull on the lights, but I found that the knob was already in the "on" position. My heart sank. I was disgusted with myself. I had left my lights on for many hours, and now my battery was totally dead.

For a few minutes, I sat in my car feeling frustrated. Then I had a sudden burst of hope. I remembered that I had bought a set of jumper cables several months ago, and it was in the trunk of my car still waiting to be used. As you probably know, a set of jumper cables consists of two parallel cables with clamps at each end. By clamping one end to a "live" battery in someone else's car and the other end to the dead battery in your own car, you can "borrow" enough power to start your car's engine.

So, I went to my associate, Bill Douglas, and he drove his car up very close to mine. We hooked up the jumper cables. He started his engine, then I turned the ignition key in my car, and vroooom! My engine started right up. I was soon on my way with the car running fine.

When our spiritual batteries run down, we need a spiritual "jumper cable." Often, we draw so much on our spiritual batteries without them being regenerated—that our batteries go dead.

How many times this happens in our lives! How many times we are the victims of dead spiritual batteries. No power. No progress. No light. No sound. Our lives have come to a standstill. The spark has gone out of them. There is no music coming out of our spiritual radios. Everything is dead.

That is precisely when we need a spiritual jumper cable to give us spark and to get things going again. That's when we need to borrow some spiritual power from Him who said, "All authority in heaven and on earth has been given to me" (Matthew 28:18).

Did you ever have the experience of a dead spiritual battery? Is all the power gone now?

By faith, use your spiritual jumper cable today. Borrow some of His power. Remember, His power is absolutely unlimited.

God wants to share His power with you.

Today.

Right now.

THE LOVING FATHER

It has been fun to be a father! Still is! It's been great fun to have the "second blessing" too; that is, to be a grandfather. How good can it get? When I count my blessings, I start with three children (Joy, Don, and Tim) and eight grandchildren. The latest grandchild, Ian, I'm happy to say, is only two years old.

What a joy it has been to watch them all from the time of their births until the present. I have marveled as they took their first steps, as they mumbled their first words, and as they, with unrestrained curiosity, examined everything in sight. I have been humbled by their unquestioning trust and by their unstudied genuineness. I have learned something of what Jesus meant when He said, "Let the children come to me, and do not hinder them; for to such belongs the kingdom of heaven" (Matthew 19:14).

Yes, it is a joy to be a father whether the "children" are four years old or forty. But, frankly, the assignment of fatherhood still staggers me. It is humbling to realize that the highest concept of God we have is that *He* is like a father. Try that on for size! And, it is God who makes the analogy.

That's what the familiar story of the prodigal son is all about. The restless son asks his father for an early inheritance, takes off for the nearest big city, blows his money on a perpetual swinging party, ends up feeding pigs, realizes he has made a fool of himself, and finally heads for home to be greeted by his loving and forgiving father (Luke 15:11–24).

It is the father, not the prodigal son, who is the real hero of the story. The father is a stand-in example of the love and forgiveness and patience of God. That's why it is such a humbling experience to be a father.

As humbling as it is, it is also a great joy to be a father. But the greatest joy of all is to know that God is a loving Father, to know that the best of my love and my forgiveness is multiplied millions and millions of times till it gets to the heavenly Father level.

Not long before his death, Philip asked Jesus this question, "Lord, show us the Father and we shall be satisfied." Jesus replied to His disciple, "Have I been with you so long, and yet you do not know me, Philip? *He who has seen me has seen the Father*" (John 14:8, 9).

There you have it. God is just like Jesus Christ. When you have seen Jesus Christ, you have seen the Father.

That's good enough for me. I can live and die with that assurance.

WHY DO GOOD PEOPLE SUFFER?

One morning several years ago, just before my open-heart surgery, I was lying in bed feeling sorry for myself. So, I flipped on the television near my bed. A doctor was interviewing a fifteen-year-old girl who had suffered all her life from diseased kidneys. As this lovely, blue-eyed girl, with courageous candor, shared her suffering, I had two immediate thoughts. First, how grateful I should be after a full life stretching more than seventy years—instead of feeling sorry about my pending operation.

The second thought is actually a very old philosophical question: Why does God allow good people to suffer? Here was this darling, charming girl explaining, with her impish grin, how she had to empty her dialysis bag four times a day in order to stay alive. She had already been the recipient of one transplanted kidney, but it functioned for only six months and then had to be removed. It seemed so unfair. Where was God in all this?

It is a baffling question. Why does God allow good people to suffer? O yes, I know, we bring *most* of our sufferings on ourselves. If we get drunk, we get hangovers. If we smoke, we are liable to suffer from cancer or heart disease. The Bible tells us that, "Whatever a man sows, that he will also reap" (Galatians 6:7).

But it is not always that simple. What about this girl who was born with bad kidneys? What about the parents who suffer when their babies die of "crib death"? What about the likes of Eric Liddell, the famous Scottish Olympic runner and Christian missionary, who died a painful death from a brain tumor while wasting away in a Japanese concentration camp? And we could all supply many more examples from experience.

Down in the cathedral of the soul, it raises serious doubts. How can a gracious God allow good people to suffer? It would be easy just to say that God is insensitive, that He is not really as good and loving a God as we thought He was. But this answer produces nothing but despair.

The better way is to take the path of faith. We can believe that God is a good and loving God even though we do not understand why things happen as they do. Some day we will understand everything from God's loving point of view. We will then see that there was purpose all the time. A Christlike God calls us to walk by faith and not by sight.

The apostle Paul, who knew the pain of unjust suffering first-hand, gives us words of encouragement—

"In everything God works for good with those who love him, who are the called according to his purpose" (Romans 8:28).

THE CHALLENGER

I just couldn't help it.

I sobbed out loud.

There, on the TV screen, was the President of the United States embracing the bereaved family members of the astronauts killed when the spacecraft Challenger blew up seventy-three seconds after lift-off from the launching pad at Cape Canaveral, Florida.

Before that, there was an even sadder vision. That was seeing the parents and the sister of the teacher-astronaut, Christine McCullough, as they excitedly viewed the launching. Unbelieving, I watched as their expressions changed from ecstasy and wide-eyed jubilation into blinding tears of despair, agony, and shock.

Yes, I sobbed out loud.

That was a long day for me. I was drained, saddened, and disillusioned.

When the space program started, I was up before dawn to watch and to cheer when the spacecraft took off. I stayed by the TV waiting for every bit of news about the flight. But, particularly as the Shuttle Program emerged, and as one flight after another was launched successfully, I began to lose interest. On some of the later shuttle flights, I ignored the launch completely and went fishing instead. I had become blasé. It was routine. I wasn't ready for this horrible tragedy. None of us were. A glorious dream had turned into a horrible nightmare.

As time wore on, I began to ask myself whether, out of this catastrophe, God might have something to say to me, some spiritual message I needed to hear. Two reminders began to imprint themselves on my mind.

First, this tragedy reminds us that we are very, very finite. We are merely human. We are very, very mortal. We are extremely imperfect. As far as the space program was concerned,

I had forgotten all this. I had come to take it all for granted. Old hat. No sweat. We've got it made.

But it is always fatal to forget the finite. "Let any one who thinks that he stands take heed lest he fall" (1 Corinthians 10:12).

Second, this tragedy reminds us that we must put our trust in God who is Infinite, Immortal, and Perfect. He holds the whole world in His hand. God's Word speaks clearly to us.

"Trust in the Lord with all thine heart and lean not on thine own understanding, in all thy ways acknowledge him, and he will direct thy paths" (Proverbs 3:6 KJV).

"Seek first his kingdom and his righteousness . . ." (Matthew 6:33).

"God is our refuge and strength, a very present help in trouble" (Psalm 46:1).

Out of tragedy, God can speak to us.

Even so, even yet, when my memory gives a replay of the heart-rending scenes of the Challenger disaster, a great sadness fills my heart, my throat tightens, and inwardly—

I sob.

Dear You

WHAT ARE YOU LOOKING FOR?

What are you looking for?

That is the question Jesus asked two of John the Baptist's disciples who had been following Him. But it is a profound question we all have to face every day. What are we actually looking for in life? What *should* we be looking for? It is all too easy to be looking for "fool's gold." Most people are.

What are you looking for?

Security? Nothing wrong with that. All of us want to have enough money to pay our bills, to have sufficient for food and shelter and doctors and the other essentials of living. We all want to feel that we have accumulated enough to live out our days without having to go begging. We all want to have some measure of security, at least enough so that we can provide a decent burial for ourselves without imposing on relatives and friends. Surely, that is not wanting too much.

But if that's all we are looking for, we are aiming far too low. I've seen people make a god out of security. It's all they can think about, all they can talk about, all they ever work for. There is no security to be found in making a god out of security.

What are you looking for?

Recognition and prestige? Nothing wrong with that.

What's wrong with wanting to be an influential person? Who doesn't want to be considered a good, kind, capable person? Nobody wants to be thought of as a "slob," that's for sure.

We should all want to use our God-given talents and God-given time to the fullest. But if it is *only* for self-centered ambition, then it is a low goal and a bad aim.

What are you looking for?

The abundant life? Yes, indeed! Now, you're on target. Now, you're in business. Jesus said, "I am come that you might have life and that you might have it more abundantly" (John 10:10 KJV).

Again and again Jesus affirms that He came to bring us a life with the "abundant" dimension. It is a life that gives us what we all hunger for—peace. This life gives us peace with ourselves, peace with others, and, above all, peace with God. Paul defines it as "the peace of God which passes all understanding" (Philippians 4:7).

And, best of all, that life is available. It is "up for grabs."

What are you looking for?

Dear You

THE SEARCH FOR MEANING

There is a message which all of us need to hear "loud and clear" every day: that despite all the bewildering and painful appearances to the contrary, life really does have meaning and purpose.

For, if life doesn't have meaning and purpose, why sweat it? Why take the bumps and bruises, the heartaches and headaches? Why suffer through the pushing and the pummelling? Why gasp for breath and continue treading water while not even knowing which way to swim?

You have wondered about the meaning of life, and so have I. Sometimes it can get downright depressing. It seems that Shakespeare experienced this. He has one of his characters give this depressing analysis, "Life is a tale, told by an idiot, full of sound and fury, signifying nothing."

Victor Frankl, the noted Viennese psychiatrist, survived the Holocaust to affirm that not only does life have meaning and purpose, but also that health, happiness, and even survival, depend upon holding such a belief.

Frankl found this out the hard way. Because he was a Jew living in Hitler's "Third Reich," he was put into a concentration camp. There he saw, and personally suffered, the hardships and horrors we have all heard about. With his trained clinical eye, he watched the harrowing struggle of people to stay alive.

Frankl observed that when people would die in the concentration camp, and while their bodies were still warm, other prisoners would grab their shoes, their coats, even leftover morsels of food. Life was incredibly precarious. Many just gave up and died.

But of more interest to Victor Frankl were those for whom life remained precious, those who clung to life tenaciously, despite the overwhelming odds against them. Why? Frankl discovered in this life-and-death situation that those who survived the inhuman ordeal were people who somehow continued to believe that there was meaning and purpose to life.

After Frankl was finally liberated at the end of the war, he wrote a book entitled, *Man's Search for Meaning*. His basic affirmation was that there is great healing power, and great survival power, in the belief that life has real meaning. He wrote that the person who is happiest and most wholesome through all the tribulations of life is the person who is convinced that life has purpose.

This is nothing new to the Christian. The apostle Paul assured us of this truth long ago. He strongly affirms it: "And we know that in all things God works for the good of those who love him, who have been called according to *his purpose*" (Romans 8:28 NIV).

Knowing this, staying alive makes sense.

Knowing this brings healing and happiness.

TELL-TALE WORDS

I have been thinking a lot lately about the power of words.

I've noticed that mothers are often very clever is using, and choosing, the right words. For example, it is eight-thirty in the evening and little Johnny sits in front of the television, enraptured by the program. Mom knows it is Johnny's bed time, but she also knows that Johnny doesn't want to go to bed. She knows that he is having a good time now, but if he stays up too late, he will be grumpy and out of sorts the next morning. Hmmmmmmmm.

Mom knows she must choose her words carefully. In a tender voice, she asks, "Johnny, do you want to be a good boy and go to bed?" Johnny wants to be a good boy, all right, but he surely doesn't want to go to bed! Still, he might well go to bed now to demonstrate to his Mom what a good boy he is.

What an enormous difference the choice of words can make in our relationships with other people. What a difference even one word can make: "I *love* you" or "I *hate* you." "I *like* you" or "I *dislike* you." "I *admire* you" or "I *despise* you." That one word between the "I" and the "you" makes all the difference in the meaning of the sentence—and in the reaction to it!

Words have the power to lift us up or put us down. They have the power to make us happy or sad. They have the power to build up or destroy.

There are only twenty-six letters in the English alphabet. It is the way in which these twenty-six letters are juggled around into words and sentences that makes the difference. But, of course, it is really the juggler of those letters who makes the difference. We are the jugglers of those letters and we are the editors of the words they form. And in the final analysis, words come from what is in the heart of the editor.

Jesus puts it better: "Out of the abundance of the heart the mouth speaks" (Matthew 12:34). Words are the verbalized heart-life of the editing self. Words are the always-revealing expression of the inner being. Our words are what usually tell other people who we really are.

If I am going to say the right thing, the good thing, and the loving thing, then I have to be right and good and loving in my heart. To make this happen, I must have the spiritual input of God's Word filling my heart. Most of all, I must have Christ in my heart. He is the "Word . . . made flesh" (John 1:14 KJV) dwelling among us. If He fully dwells in my heart, the words I use will be edited by His inner Presence, and the words that come out of my mouth will bring healing and blessing to others because they are not really my words at all.

They are His.

THE GOOD SAMARITAN

It is so hard to remember that, "It is more blessed to give than to receive" (Acts 20:35). We need to be reminded of this fact all the time. It is a lesson that keeps eluding us because it simply goes against everything in human nature.

Somehow, there is a subtle, sneaky way our minds work to create an inner attitude that says it's better to be a "receiver" than a "giver." This is certainly not a new idea. It's as old as self-centeredness, which means that it's as old as humanity itself. And, of course, the world around us blasts us with the same message every hour of every day. It is "taken for granted" by most people that whatever brings pleasure or possessions to them is automatically "good."

But contradicting all that is "obvious," Jesus says: "It is more blessed to give than to receive."

You know something? I'll bet the Good Samaritan was a very happy man. He was a "giver." As a Samaritan, he was hated and despised—and considered "inferior" by the Jews of the day. But when a Jew who had been mugged and robbed was found lying by the side of the road in a pool of his own blood, it was the despised Samaritan who came to his rescue.

Two Jewish religious leaders passed by this badly injured man before the Good Samaritan arrived. But they were too preoccupied with their religious responsibilities to stop and help this dying man. Besides, the mugged man was a pathetic and disturbing sight. And this was a dangerous, high-crime area. The only prudent thing to do was to keep on moving and get out of there as quickly as possible.

But the Samaritan had a deeper urge than prudence. Ignoring his own personal safety, he poured wine on the open wounds of the injured man. He then soothed the pain with oil and covered the wounds with cloth (probably torn from his own garments). The Samaritan was covered with grime and blood as he lifted the man onto his donkey. Holding the man on the donkey, he walked alongside him to the nearest inn, where he stayed and ministered to him through the night. In the morning, he paid for the man's expenses and left only after promising to pay for any further expenses that might be incurred (Luke 10:30–35).

What a beautiful morning it was to the Samaritan. I'm sure there must have been a peaceful look on his face as he rode along. Sure, he'd blown his "schedule" by making this unplanned stop. But the Good Samaritan was not behind schedule. He was right on schedule. He was right on time.

Somewhere, somehow, sometime, this "outcast" Samaritan had discovered that "Joy is an inside job." He had learned and remembered one of life's most vital, and most elusive, truths—

"It is more blessed to give than to receive" (Acts 20:35).

A Sermon from a Salmon

Years ago I got a sermon from a salmon.

Here's how it happened. While riding on a ferryboat to Galiano Island in British Columbia, I struck up a conversation with Mr. Thompson, a dignified and friendly gentlemen who served as the Chief Clerk for the City of Vancouver.

I said, "I've heard that after a salmon is spawned, it will swim out into the ocean, and that after an extended time something happens inside the brain of the salmon, and it will then have the overwhelming urge to return to the place where it was spawned. The salmon will swim along the coast, find the right harbor, the right river, the right stream; and finally it will get back to the very spot where it started out. How in the world does the salmon do that?" I added, hoping it would be taken as a joke, "After all, the salmon is underwater all the way, and it has no periscope."

Mr. Thompson chuckled, thought a bit, then replied, "Yes, that is true, but it is even more remarkable than that. An experiment was recently carried out in which salmon eggs were removed from the stream where they had been laid and were put into another stream some distance away." Thompson then added with a questioning grin, "When the salmon grows up and swims out to the ocean and finally swims back home, which location will it swim to? Will it swim to the place where the eggs were laid—or to the place where they had been moved to?"

I paused for a moment, then I gave what I thought was the only sensible answer, "The salmon will swim back to the place where the eggs had been transported, of course. That's where the salmon actually turned into a fish and got to know its environment."

"Wrong!" said Mr. Thompson. "The salmon will swim back to the original place where the eggs were laid."

I was dumbfounded then, and I still am, by this uncanny built-in guidance system of the salmon.

What a sermon on the guidance of God! If God provides such marvelous guidance for a fish, there is certainly nothing fishy about believing that He can provide guidance for us. We are far more important to God than any fish. We are created in God's own image.

God only knows how much we need His wise and loving guidance as we try to find our way through the jungle of "this world." And, thank God, He has personally promised His guidance.

"I will guide thee with mine eye" (Psalm 32:8 KJV).

SPIRITUAL COVERUP

Did you ever rationalize sin in your life?

Well, take heart, you are in good company.

Take, for example, Aaron, the first High Priest of Israel. He was the man chosen by God to be the "mouthpiece" for the stuttering Moses. He was not only the spokesman for Moses but was the "second in command" in Moses' absence.

Moses was up on the Mount getting the commandments from God. Pretty serious business. But while he was on this sacred—and prolonged—mission, not-so-funny business was going on at the encampment of the Israelites, where Aaron was now in charge. The people were getting restless, not only because of Moses' long absence, but also because they were getting a hankering for a false god and all the sensuousness that went along with it.

Aaron, who apparently got caught up in the same spirit after awhile, went along with this pagan urge and even became the man in charge of it. He organized and motivated the people to gather up their golden earrings and other gold ornaments. They brought him a huge haul which he had melted down and then fashioned, with the tools of the time, into an enormous golden calf.

The people, who were already clamoring for such a god, were told by Aaron that this, the great golden calf, was their new god. He called for a time of revelry.

At that time, Moses came back from the Mount and saw what was going on. He immediately dashed the engraved tablets on the ground. Hot with anger, Moses yelled at Aaron, "What did these people do to you that you led them into such great sin?" (Exodus 32:21 NIV).

Please try to keep a straight face as you hear his answer: "Do not be angry, my lord. You know how prone *these people* are to evil. They said to me, 'Make us gods who will go before us. As for this fellow Moses who brought us up out of Egypt, we don't know what has happened to him.' So I told them, 'Whoever has any golden jewelry, take it off.' Then they gave me the gold, and *I threw it into the fire, and out came this calf!"* (Exodus 32:22–24 NIV).

So you see, rationalizing sin is nothing new. And it is with us still: "I committed adultery because my wife did not meet my needs." "I divorced my husband because he was too dominating." "I have to cheat in my business because if you don't cheat, you don't stay in business." "I stick up banks because my parents didn't discipline me." "I am fat because of a glandular condition." I'm sure you can all add more examples.

Rationalizing our sin is a surefire formula for continued defeat. It is an absolute block to spiritual victory.

The prodigal son, one of my favorite Bible characters, had a real recovery because he had a real confession. He said to his father, "I have sinned against heaven and before you; I am no longer worthy to be called your son" (Luke 15:21).

In our hearts, we know that rationalizing sin is phony. A phony self can never experience a *real* blessing.

Where there is a cover-up, there is no spiritual pick-up.

THE EMPTINESS OF SUCCESS

One evening I happened to see Merv Griffin conducting an interview with Kirk Douglas. The famous actor described the poverty that had gripped his early life. He told of his struggle to become an actor in the city of New York. And one of the incidents he described particularly stuck with me.

One evening, Kirk Douglas and another aspiring young actor were sitting together in Central Park. Full of ambition and dreams, Douglas pointed to the top floor, the twenty-fifth, of a very expensive Manhattan hotel and said, "Some day I am going to live in the most expensive suite up there. I am going to be right up there where those lights are."

Then Kirk Douglas paused and, in his own distinctive, dramatic way, he spoke to Griffin and the television audience as though he were divulging a great secret or revelation. He said, "You know, as time went on, I did live up there in the best suite on the twenty-fifth floor. But you know, when I did live there, I found it wasn't as much fun looking down on Central Park as it was being in the park looking up at the lights on the twenty-fifth floor."

I have heard this same theme and thought from many other successful actors and actresses. They hoped, they dreamed, they worked to become stars. When they did "make it," there was not nearly the satisfaction they'd expected.

Oh, perhaps at first the flush of "success" was exciting and exhilarating. But in the long run, they felt somehow "empty"; they felt that something was missing.

The reason for this is simple but often slippery: fame and money do not satisfy the deepest needs in our hearts. I do not mean to knock the desire for success. But real success is a spiritual experience.

Jesus says to us all, "Man shall not live by bread alone, but by every word that proceeds from the mouth of God"

(Matthew 4:4). Physical needs are important and their satisfaction is necessary, but taking care of the physical is not enough.

We need a word from God. We need spiritual food. We cannot *really* live on bread (or anything else that money can buy) *alone.*

From personal experience I have found that if I do not read the Bible daily, I begin to lose my fellowship with the Author. My faith becomes weaker without that spiritual input. I need the assurance of His forgiveness and the promise of His guidance each day. I need to hear Him say, again and again—

"I have come that they may have life, and have it to the full" (John 10:10 NIV).

A New Face

Some years ago a touching true story was told in a national magazine about a beautiful and bright nurse. This young lady's life seemed all in front of her and the future looked rosy to her. Then, without warning or preparation, her life was dramatically and permanently changed.

She had a head-on collision with a huge truck and the lower part of her face was completely torn off by the crushing impact. Her appearance was so horrible and grotesque that it shocked the police and hospital staff who attended her. Later, two girl scouts selling cookies door-to-door ran away screaming after she appeared at the door. Her husband couldn't handle it. He divorced her. She was all alone, ugly, injured, and hopeless. No wonder, at this point, she cried, again and again, "Why me, God?"

But the story does not end there—in her deep despair. There was a considerate, courageous, and determined young plastic surgeon at Elendorf Air Force Hospital who would not let her quit. With patience, skill, and even ingenuity, he rebuilt the entire lower part of her face. It took seven years and an incredible thirty-five operations in all.

But now, this same young nurse, the near-monstrosity that literally scared children, is once more an attractive woman. But the story does not end here either.

Through the long haul of treatment, surgery, and rehabilitation, the character and personality of this valiant young nurse had shone through the scars and deformations and had reached the heart of the physician, a bachelor at the time. In the end, he was so attracted to her looks as well as to her "person" that he asked her to marry him. She had also fallen in love with the doctor. They are now husband and wife. Now she says things have worked out so wonderfully in her life that she has the answer to the agonizing question which once had dominated her life, "Why me, God?"

The dedicated physician had created a new face and brought beauty, hope, satisfaction, and happiness into a life crushed by despair. This reminds me of another physician—the "Great Physician." Jesus Christ takes our sin-mangled lives and creates a new person. With patience and love, He carves out for us a new inner face.

Listen, once more, to the great assurance that the apostle Paul gives us concerning Christ's creative work: "If any man be in Christ, he is a new creature; old things are passed away. Behold, all things are become new" (2 Corinthians 5:17 KJV).

Let us surrender our lives to the Great Physician so that He can do a job of creative surgery on us.

BEING PREPARED

I could hardly believe the news report. In December, 1986, a British tanker, the 26,000 ton *Syneta*, struck a tall rock off the coast of Ireland and sank with the loss of all crewmen aboard.

The Board of Inquiry found that the Captain had misjudged the ship's position. The *Syneta* crashed into Skruder Rock, which juts 531 feet out of the water and is also marked by an operating lighthouse. The weather was perfect; the visibility was excellent. Rescue efforts were fatally delayed because the crew radioed the wrong position of their ship. The Board of Inquiry found that the ship had faulty radar equipment and, for its one "lifeboat," an inflatable raft that could accommodate only six people.

What a tragedy! Can you imagine any sane person going out to sea, with all its perils, in a ship like that? Think of it. Here you have a supposedly modern, well-equipped vessel running into a massive rock that stands over 500 feet above the ocean. And has a lighthouse flashing on it! Here you have a situation with clear skies and a well-known rock that is marked on all the nautical charts of the area. Here you have rescue ships arriving too late because the crew gave them a wrong position due to faulty radar. And when the ship went down, here you have the crew with a virtually worthless lifeboat to fall back on. Absolutely amazing, isn't it? Almost unbelievable.

What a contrast is the delightful trip I took on the *Canberra*, a Greek ship cruising from Ireland to Montreal, Canada. For nine days my brother, Doug, and I sailed through rough seas and overcast skies. Since both of us are hearty sailors who love the sea, we had a great time standing in the bow of the vessel, letting the spray from the huge waves crash over our heads.

One of the ship's officers told me that we would be entering the Belle Isle straits the next morning at six o'clock, so I was up before dawn peering into the mist to catch the first sight of land. Suddenly the mist cleared, and there we were, right in the middle of the straits. I thought, What a fine ship! *What a crew! What a wonderful trip! And . . . what a captain!*

We are all sailing out into the open sea with all its uncertainties and dangers. There are rocks and storms out there. Hidden icebergs and subtle dangers lurk out there. It can be a fun trip or a fatal trip.

Preparation is what makes the difference. We must prepare our hearts to center on the Unseen, not on the "seen." "For what is seen is temporary, but what is unseen is eternal" (2 Corinthians 4:18).

We must center our hearts on Jesus Christ, "The Captain of our salvation." He is "The Way, The Truth, and The Life" (John 14:6). He is the Navigator! We must center our hearts in the will of God and not in our own will. "Not my will be done, but thine."

Then we can shout with confidence, "Anchors away!"

FROZEN FEET

I was deeply moved by a newspaper story of a young serviceman who had both feet amputated in a hospital in New Mexico.

This young black man was driving through Raton, New Mexico, when he ran out of gas and out of cash. He had a checkbook and he carried identification, but no one would cash his check. He tried all the banks in town. All refused.

The cold winter night was closing in, but the serviceman was still stranded. No money for gas and no money for a motel room. In desperation he curled up and slept in his frigid car. In the morning, his feet would not move. They were frostbitten.

Help finally came on that cold morning in New Mexico. But it was too late!

Both feet had to be amputated.

Now a thought kept haunting me. A question that will not go away. But it isn't the question, Why didn't the church help him? That's simple. He never asked anyone in the church.

But why didn't he ask one of the churches for help? That's what haunts me. Why didn't he ask? Did he assume that church people didn't care? That they didn't want to be annoyed? Perhaps he was too proud to ask. Perhaps he never thought of it. I don't know. But as I say, it keeps haunting me. It won't let me go.

It haunts me as I picture those stumps sticking out of the man's khaki trousers. It haunts me as I see him ushered out of the military, a cripple for life. It haunts me as I see him as a lonely kid in a lonely city going from bank to bank. It haunts me as I see him shivering in his car waiting hopefully for the sun to come up. It haunts me as I see him walking to his car but being carried out on a stretcher. It haunts me as I wonder if he cried during that lonely night.

Somehow the church must be on the lookout for people who are hurting. Somehow, we must learn to love people enough to help them where it hurts. I feel guilty that this young serviceman did not come to any church for help. The churches in Raton should feel guilty, and all the Christian churches everywhere should feel guilty about this.

But do you know what haunts me most about this? This is the painful question that makes me search my own soul—

Would *I* have cashed his check?

DIAMONDS IN THE ROUGH

All of us have enjoyed the musical, "My Fair Lady."

As the story begins, Professor Henry Higgins and a close friend of his, a retired military officer, are engaged in a rather heated discussion. Professor Higgins is arguing that environmental influences are paramount in determining a person's character and personality. Higgins, a renowned scholar of languages, is even claiming that he is able to identify an individual's exact geographical and social class origins by merely listening to how he uses, and pronounces, the English language. Higgins' friend, a fellow member of their exclusive social circle, is, to say the least, skeptical.

So, they take to the streets of London. And Higgins impressively backs up his claim by accurately determining, from the "accents" of various people, their actual position in society and the neighborhoods in which they were raised. Among those they meet is a scruffy, disheveled flower girl, Eliza Doolittle, whose coarse "Cockney" accent clearly reveals her lower-class London origin. Her clothes are ragged and her language is crude. She possesses none of the "social graces." On the social scale, she is at the lowest rung of the ladder.

To Higgins, this young "guttersnipe" (as he refers to her) represents a kind of ultimate challenge to his theories. He bets his friend that in one year he can turn this coarse and unschooled young lady into someone acceptable to London "high society." Higgins' friend thinks it preposterous. The bet is gladly accepted.

It takes some doing, but Professor Higgins is able to persuade the girl to come to his lavish home for a year of concentrated training. His housekeeper reluctantly accepts young Eliza as a guest in the home. The experiment begins.

It's hard work and difficult going all the way. During the year, Miss Doolittle is taught how to speak "proper" English, which Higgins considers of primary importance if she is to "pass" for an upper-class debutante. You remember, "The rain in Spain stays mainly on the plain."

She is also taught how to walk with sophistication, how to dance with elegance, and how to demonstrate all the social graces. It is uphill all the way. More than once, Higgins is on the verge of quitting. So is Eliza. But they both persevere. Gradually, Eliza develops into a lovely, "cultured" young woman.

The big day arrives. Higgins proudly introduces her to the highest London "society." She is an instant sensation. The young bachelors wonder, "Where has she been?" Her beauty and charm take everyone by storm and leaves Higgins glowing in his greatest "success."

Only then does he realize that he, himself, has actually fallen in love with this one-time "guttersnipe." The lifelong bachelor in Higgins wants to be rid of her now that the experiment is over, but he ends up singing, wistfully, "I've grown accustomed to her face."

In each of us there is a beautiful person who can come forth through the influence of God's power and God's "training."

Our hearts, our thinking, our acts, and our desires may all be of the "slum" variety, but God can change all that. Peter, the coarse and cowardly fisherman, became, through God's power, the rocklike apostle of Christ.

In each of us there is "a diamond in the rough."

Dear You

A SERMON FROM A SEED

Only God can make a tree!

Especially a tree like the Great Sequoia, "General Sherman," which stands in Sequoia National Park in California. Millions of people have stood at the base of this giant of the forest and looked up in awe at its majestic heights. And no wonder.

The General Sherman is 272 feet tall, has a base more than one hundred feet across, and is estimated to weigh over 2,000 tons. It is the most massive tree ever found on the planet Earth (or any other planet, for that matter!). And the General Sherman has been there for a very long time. Over 3,000 years, in fact. That means it was a seedling over a thousand years before the birth of Jesus Christ.

What a grand tree! What a marvelous product of God's creation! What an inspiring sight!

But its spectacular size is not what is most inspiring about the General Sherman. Not what it is but how it came to be, that is the most impressive thing. It staggers the mind.

Listen. This huge tree came from a tiny seed—and I do mean *tiny*. The seed of a Giant Sequoia actually weighs only 1/6000 of an ounce. That's one six-thousandth of an ounce. Take an ounce of material and divide it into six thousand parts and see how big each part is—if you can manage to do it!

Yes, the seed that grew to be the General Sherman was a very tiny seed, but *potentially* it was a very mighty seed. Built into that minute seed, due to the infinite intelligence and power of God, was the potential to become the greatest of all the Great Sequoias.

God has done the same for us. Into our tiny, transitory lives, He has built a mighty *potential*. It is not what we are, but what we can become that is truly amazing. It is the incredible *potential* that lies dormant there. "As many as received him, to them gave he power to become the sons of God" (John 1:12 KJV). The Godlike potential is there.

Peter was *actually* a coarse, unlearned, loud-mouthed fisherman with a streak of cowardliness to boot; but *potentially* he was a fearless, loving apostle of Jesus Christ.

Saul of Tarsus was *actually* an angry, bitter persecutor of the early Christians; but *potentially* he was the proclaimer of the gospel to the gentile world.

Matthew was *actually* a greedy and hated tax-collector; but *potentially* he was an apostle and the author of the first gospel, the story of the life of Christ.

All of us are an *"actual"* and *"potential."* If God can make an infinitesimal Sequoia seed that has within it the potential to be a "General Sherman," then He certainly can give no less potential to those creatures who are made in His own image. For us, He has done even more. The *potential* is there! Believe it!

"(He is) able to do far more abundantly than all that we ask or think" (Ephesians 3:20).

BUILD HIGHER AND STRONGER

My son, Tim, and I stood on the shore and nervously watched the stormy Pacific Ocean batter the Venice Pier with its huge, power-packed waves. It was an awesome sight.

The water is usually calm here, and the surface is normally about twenty feet below the deck of the pier. But now the water was angry and it was booming way up over the end of the pier. The surging waves roared along, hitting the piles and sending clouds of spray into the air.

Before our unbelieving eyes, the ramp leading up onto the pier (on which we had been standing just minutes before), suddenly crumbled. Where the shore end of the pier used to be, there was now just a gaping hole. The waves had undermined the concrete, and the ramp had collapsed of its own weight. It was frightening to see the sea unleash that kind of awesome power.

But the storm toll was even worse elsewhere. The Santa Monica Pier, as well as other piers, stormwalls, and breakwaters up and down the coast, were battered to pieces. The shoreline was littered with the debris. Houses were torn apart and tossed into the churning surf. As the storm continued, people close to the shore waited and worried. It reminded me of the title of a book, *The Cruel Sea.*

When the storm finally abated, officials began to discuss the issue of recovery and reconstruction. Their assessment was unanimous: "Next time we will build higher and stronger."

They had learned their lesson. They had seriously misjudged the power of the sea at its worst. They had underestimated the storm.

We can all get a sermon from the storm. The ocean is not always calm and peaceful. Neither is life. But, too often, we smugly live on, taking for granted that the sea of life will remain calm and peaceful forever. But then comes the storm, and we are terribly unprepared for the raging waves. We crumble.

Jesus tells us about a man who made the same mistake. He built his house upon the sand, and when the storm came, it wiped out that house. "And great was the fall of it" (Matthew 7:27).

The lesson is very clear. We had better build our lives with the inevitable storm always in mind, or we will build poorly indeed. Through the Word of God and through prayer, we must build into our lives the strength to withstand the mightiest storms of life.

"Next time we must build higher and stronger."

LOVING AND LOSING

"Love does not demand its own way" (1 Corinthians 13:5 TLB).

That's what the apostle Paul says. And he's right, of course. Love is not self-centered. It is willing to surrender to the feelings of others. Sometimes we have to find this out the hard way.

Some years ago, I invited my eldest son and his wife for dinner. Their enthusiasm was boundless. My son's wife invited her mother and father to come along. My wife invited her mother. The "intimate" dinner I had in mind was fast going "out the window." (The price was going up fast, too.)

I had planned to take them to my favorite continental restaurant, but the others all agreed they'd rather go to a certain Chinese restaurant. I said, "Sure, I'll go along with whatever everyone else wants to do." But inwardly, I was furious! I thought to myself, *This dinner is my idea in the first place. I'm paying the bill, and, yet, here I am, being pushed aside and completely ignored. Here I am, being taken advantage of instead of being appreciated.* Boy, was I doing a slow burn.

But—ha, ha, ha—I got my revenge before the evening was over. I grumbled, I pouted, I gave them all the silent treatment, and, with inward glee, I made everyone feel uncomfortable and miserable. I was delighted with my "Oscar" performance. For a little while.

But later the same evening, riding home with my son, I began to feel guilty about the way I'd acted. I tried to explain. But my son blurted out abruptly, "Dad, let's face it. You blew it."

He was right. I did blow it. My attitude was self-centered, not loving. I was demanding my own way and making it unpleasant for others if I didn't get my own way. But God says to us, "Love does not demand its own way."

I felt out-of-joint with God and with the others. I only found peace again when I went to all of them and said I was sorry.

Love brings victory through surrender. It does not demand its own way. The only way you ever really "find yourself" is to—

Lose yourself.

TOP OFF YOUR TANK

Recently this brief, crisp radio transmission could be heard among the din of radio signals over the San Fernando Valley: "Tango . . . Victor . . . Four . . . Just lost . . ."

The desperate voice sending that unfinished message was that of Gary Powers. Powers, you may remember, became a prisoner of the Soviets and the center of a major international controversy when his high-flying U-2 spy plane was shot down over the Soviet Union in 1960.

Back in the U.S. for years and working as a television news helicopter pilot in Los Angeles, Powers was returning from filming a brush fire north of Santa Barbara when the fatal crash occurred. A little earlier, Powers had radioed that he had just about enough fuel to make the one-hour-long trip back to his home base at Hollywood/Burbank Airport.

He was dead wrong. His helicopter lost power and the half-million dollar craft fell 800 feet into an open field near the Sepulveda Dam.

Investigators searched for the causes of this "Telecopter" tragedy, which killed the only passenger, KNBC-TV technician George Spears, as well as Gary Powers. They found that Powers was an experienced pilot in both fixed-wing aircraft and helicopters, that the plane's gross weight and center-of-gravity were within limits, that the helicopter had been inspected and maintained properly, and it had taken off that day with full fuel tanks.

In fact, the investigators could find no other explanation for the crash than this: "The pilot simply ran out of gas."

It is so sad because it was so unnecessary. Powers didn't have to push his luck; he didn't have to try to stretch his fuel supply to the limit in order to avoid making a stop. But he did. There are several airports between Santa Barbara and Burbank where he *could* have stopped to refuel. But instead, he tried to "save time" and squeeze by, but he just didn't have enough fuel in his tanks. As an experienced pilot he knew better, of course, but he tried to make it home with no "margin for error"!

Don't we all? How often we try to get by with too little spiritual fuel in our tanks. We don't stop to meditate, to pray, or to read God's Word. We fail to fill up with God's presence and power though they are available the whole time.

Then comes the inevitable crash. The sometimes fatal crash. And it's all so unnecessary.

Plenty of spiritual fuel is available to you. And with it, the power to stay aloft and keep going forward. Jesus says, "You shall receive power after that the Holy Spirit is come upon you" (Acts 1:8).

The fuel and the power are there.

Top off your tanks.

Today.

"They who wait for the Lord shall renew their strength, they shall mount up with wings like eagles, they shall run and not be weary, they shall walk, and not faint" (Isaiah 40:31).

FRANK THE FREELOADER

Bill was the superintendent of a large rescue mission in a huge American city. He was a fine Christian with a big heart who had the responsibility of handling a large staff that ministered to very needy men in the heart of the city. These "skid row derelicts" came to the mission daily looking for food, clothes and shelter for survival.

Frank was one of these men, a long-term alcoholic. He was a regular at the rescue mission. In fact, he was a confirmed freeloader. Day after day, year after year, Frank was there, getting whatever he could. He always had his hand out; he was always taking advantage of those who worked sacrificially at the mission, many of them volunteers. When he wasn't drunk, he was at the mission. But he never once seemed to make any effort to change.

Bill, the superintendent, finally lost his patience with Frank. One day, tired and emotionally drained by a hectic schedule, Bill took Frank aside. He said to him very firmly, "Frank, I'm disgusted with you. You have been coming in here for years. You go out and get drunk, and then you come back here every night for a free ride. You use our showers, eat our food, use our beds, take the clothes we offer, and you make no effort to give anything back. And you seem to make no effort whatever to change. I've had it with you, Frank. Please leave and don't come back."

Without saying a word, Frank walked out of the building. At the end of the day, Bill turned off his office lights and headed for the front door of the mission, thinking of the restful evening with his family that awaited him at home.

But when Bill opened the front door of the building, he was hit in the face by cold sheets of rain driven by a strong, gusty wind. Immediately the question struck him, *What about*

Frank? How can I possibly go home to a warm fire when he is out there somewhere in this storm? No way. I can't do it.

So, Bill grabbed an umbrella and ran out into the driving rain looking for Frank. Getting soaked himself, Bill scurried around the dingy downtown streets, peering through the pelting rain. Finally, he spotted a figure huddled in the narrow doorway of a deserted building, holding a newspaper over his head. Bill approached, and sure enough, it was Frank. He was shivering from the cold and wet.

Bill grabbed Frank and, looking into his eyes, said, "Frank, I want you to come back. I'm going to give you one more chance." Frank and Bill shivered together as they shared the umbrella back to the mission.

A few years after that, Bill died suddenly. The Board of Directors of the mission prayerfully considered who they could find to replace the seemingly indispensable Bill as superintendent of the mission. They unanimously agreed on one man. His name?

Frank.

Yes, Frank, the lazy, dirty, drunken freeloader. Yes, Frank, who also got "one more chance."

The potential was there all the time. That pathetic creature huddled in the rain was potentially Frank, the superintendent of the mission. Frank, the one man to carry on the great work of his predecessor, Bill.

Christ made the difference.

The potential is there in all of us. Don't give up on yourself. And the potential is there in others, too. Don't give up on others, because the apparently "hopeless case" may turn out to be another Frank.

Remember, God is not through with us yet.

"All things are possible with God."

"What a Friend"

Since I became a Christian many years ago, one of the hymns that has been dearest to my heart is "What a Friend We Have in Jesus." I am not alone. This wonderful hymn has cheered millions of Christians experiencing times of trouble. Many people going through times of discouragement and despair have been reminded by this song that we really do have a Friend in Jesus who is always there for the asking and for the trusting.

Joseph Scriven, the author of this hymn, was born in Dublin in 1820 and immigrated to Canada when he was twenty-five years of age. He made plans to be married. Scriven was a happy young man, full of optimism, with his life ahead of him. He eagerly looked forward to starting a Christian family.

Then tragedy struck and broke his heart. On the eve of their wedding day, the lovely girl he was to marry accidentally drowned.

Scriven was crushed, but he did not become bitter. Instead, he consecrated his life and fortune to Jesus Christ and to the service of other human beings. Though he was a graduate of prestigious Trinity College in Dublin, a man of education and "refinement," Scriven decided to spend his days on earth humbly serving needy people in practical ways.

One afternoon, Scriven was walking down the streets of Port Hope, where he lived. He was dressed as a plain working man, and he was carrying a saw and sawhorse used for cutting wood. A new and prosperous resident of the town, seeing Scriven, turned to another man and said, "Do you know that man? I'd like to have him cut some wood for me, too."

"But you can't get *that* man," was the reply.

"Why not?"

"Because you can afford to pay for the work."

"What?" said the newcomer, unbelieving. "You're telling

me I can't hire that man because I *can* afford to pay for his services? I've never heard of such a thing."

"That's right," said the other man. "That's Joseph Scriven. He only works for free. And he only saws wood for poor widows and orphans and sick people."

Yes, that was Joseph Scriven. He knew that Jesus was his friend and he wanted to share that friendship with others, especially with those who had great need. He was a man who had felt the crush of tragedy but who lived the reality of triumph through prayer. That's why he could write:

What a friend we have in Jesus, All our sins and griefs to bear.
What a privilege to carry, Everything to God in prayer!

O, what peace we often forfeit, O what needless pain we bear,
All, because we do not carry Everything to God in prayer!

Have we trials and temptations? Is there trouble anywhere?
We should never be discouraged, Take it to the Lord in prayer.

Can we find a friend so faithful Who will all our sorrows share?
Jesus knows our every weakness, Take it to the Lord in prayer.

Dear You

LIVING IN THE REAL WORLD

As I was taking my morning walk near the Pacific Ocean, I stopped to chat with a wealthy businessman. I have done this a number of times before, so he and I have become quite good friends. We are now able to speak frankly with each other.

And, frankly speaking, he is one of the most materialistic individuals I have ever met. His eye is on the American dollar with a consuming passion. This man is in his mid-sixties, but his future is filled with new plans and projects that will increase his wealth. His conversation is basically a materialistic monologue. But the cold truth is that if he never made another penny, he'd never be able to spend what he's accumulated already.

As soon as the greetings were over, he was off and running, telling me about his latest money-making project. Finally, I could not resist breaking in to remark, as casually as possible, "Jesus said, 'A man's life does not consist in the abundance of his possessions'" (Luke 12:15).

My friend didn't get a bit perturbed. He just replied, dogmatically, "I always try to make all the money I can, and I'm going to do it all my life." He then started pouring forth, one more time, the justifications for his preoccupation with money, but I excused myself to continue my walk.

As I walked alongside the blue sea and the white sand on that crisp but sunny morning, I felt a pang of sadness for this man who had absolutely no eye for the spiritual dimension of life. Here he was, in the sunset years of his life, and he only had eyes for the "here and now," and only for the material world. A verse of scripture popped into my mind: "While we look not at the things which are seen, but at the things which are not seen: for the things which are seen are temporal; but the things which are not seen are eternal" (2 Corinthians 4:18).

But, of course, this man is not alone. None of us has yet "arrived." It is easy to get totally caught up in the "seen" world;

all too easy to forget that the "unseen" world is the *real* world. Setting our affections on "the things of this world" is short-sightedness of the worst kind. Whenever we are beset with pain within or perplexities and problems without, our hope and strength must come from the Unseen.

The writer of the book of Hebrews gives us a summary of the trials and problems Moses had in leading the people of Israel out of Egypt. He said that Moses was able to go through the ordeals inflicted by a cruel and stubborn Pharaoh and by a mob of grumbling Israelites because—

"He endured as seeing him who is *invisible*" (Hebrews 11:27 KJV).

"Looking unto Jesus the author and finisher of our faith" (Hebrews 12:2 KJV).

LOVE THYSELF

Many times I have felt worthless. I'm sure you have, too. We need to remind ourselves often that we are worth something to God and to ourselves.

Years ago, when I was a professional counselor in the Trotter Medical Building in Los Angeles, a thirty-year-old woman came to see me at the urging of her husband. She complained of severe "friction" in her marriage and doubted whether the marriage could survive.

This woman was distinctive in that she seemed to be completely bereft of any attractive features. Now, most people have something going for them: nice eyes, hair, skin, figure, voice, laugh, wit, whatever, but at least something. This woman seemed to have no "redeeming feature" at all. She had dry, strawy hair; pimpled face; fat body; tiny, listless eyes; a squeaky voice; an unpleasant demeanor, et cetera. In addition, she was bursting with hostility toward her husband.

But she was obviously a very intelligent person. In a way, this was unfortunate. She was all-too-painfully aware of how horrible she looked and how miserably she acted. And yet, she seemed to be totally trapped in this negative pattern.

After several sessions with the wife, I had the husband come to see me. I was startled when he walked into my office because this was a man who seemed to have everything going for him. He was tall, trim, muscular, and very handsome. He had a winsome and contagious personality, a ready sense of humor, and a comfortable, confident manner. Never have I seen such a striking contrast in a couple. The contrast screamed out at you.

But one thing quickly became very clear. This man really loved his wife. Over and over, he expressed his affection for her. He was mystified that she did not seem to really accept and believe that he loved her.

In this case, the truth was quite transparent. This woman was a "classic case" of terribly low self-esteem. She could not bring herself to believe in herself. She could not bring herself to love herself. Thus, she could not believe that her husband could love her. Her tirades toward him were actually tests.

How we all need to feel that there is something lovable in us. We all need to learn to love ourselves better. Each of us needs to feel that he or she is very worthwhile, indeed.

Jesus says, "Love thy neighbor *as thyself*" (Mark 12:31 KJV). That means that neighbor-love—something we need a lot more of in this world—is a by-product of self-love. You can't have the one without the other. We cannot even become capable of truly loving another person until we have learned to love ourselves.

When the fire of self-love burns low, we can also look to the cross. The cross is a constant reminder that we are each very important to God. The clincher is this: if we are worth that much to God, we must be worth something to ourselves.

GIVE IT YOUR BEST

The Bible says, "Whatsoever thy hand findeth to do, do it with all thy might" (Ecclesiastes 9:10 KJV). What does this mean?

It means to live your life to the fullest wherever you are and whoever you are with and whatever you are doing. It means to do your best regardless of the circumstances and let the future take care of itself. It means to meet the nearest need, put yourself wholly into the challenge at hand.

John Bunyan was an uneducated man who boldly preached the gospel in England despite warnings from the authorities to desist. He was thrown in jail for his convictions. Did he sit around and mope about his fate? No! Without education, books, or any comforts, he picked up a pen and started writing. What came of this effort? One of the great works of the Christian faith, a book that has blessed the lives of millions, *Pilgrim's Progress.*

"Whatsoever thy hand findeth to do, do it with all thy might."

Jesus prayed wherever He was: out on a mountain top, in a garden, or on a lake. Jesus used the leadership He had at hand: fishermen, a tax gatherer, uneducated men, the lot.

Each of us is tempted to wish he had another job, that he lived in a more beautiful place, that his life was more interesting and stimulating. You know, "the grass is greener" somewhere else, or "I'll give it my all when the right opportunity comes along."

But God says, "Whatsoever thy hand findeth to do, do it with all thy might."

This also means give it your best shot *today.* Yesterday is gone. Tomorrow we don't have yet. God wants us to be in union with Christ and then to "live for today." That's why we sing, "Moment by moment, I'm kept in His love." Your walk with God in the future starts with the step you take today. As the ancient Chinese proverb says, "The trip of a thousand miles begins with the first step." Or as the modern American proverb puts it, "Today is the first day of the rest of your life."

Indeed, today is the only day you ever really have. So, *today*, give it your all wherever you are, and leave the future to God. It's in good hands!

A Heartbeat Away

Shock treatment!

I was enjoying a delightful lunch and rich fellowship with Christians in the arts, media, and professional sports. There were ten people sitting at my table and everyone was having a splendid time sharing experiences and renewing acquaintances. The food was excellent, too, and we were all "digging in."

Suddenly, over the buzz of conversation, an urgent grunt roared out. All movement and talking ceased instantly. Everyone sensed that something was terribly wrong. Pale faces and startled eyes followed the sound. Something desperate was happening.

There was tall, powerful Keith Erickson, the well-known former professional basketball player and now sports commentator, standing behind a man who was choking on a piece of chicken. Keith had already lifted the man into an upright position. Using the Heimlich maneuver, Keith, with his arms around the man's body and his fists pushing against the diaphragm, was now vigorously and repeatedly yanking the man toward his own body. Each time he did this, Keith let out a grunt. The sound filled the deathly silent room. But the victim did not grunt, cough, breathe, or even wheeze. He was getting no air at all and was obviously about to pass out.

All of us were choking with the stricken man. All of us were fighting for our lives. All of us were tensing up with each of Keith's grunts, trying to expel that potentially fatal bite.

Suddenly, Keith stopped. The man took several gasping, desperate breaths while a white-faced Keith continued to support his body. Then Keith bent over and asked him anxiously, "Are you all right?"

The man raised his head and lifted his hands in a gesture of praise to God. A roar of applause broke out. We all stood up with cheers and praise. And then, prayer. It had been a real-life triumph over tragedy.

When Keith Erickson got up to address the luncheon guests, he omitted his customary introductory jokes. After a brush with death like that, it would have seemed like laughing in the intensive care ward of a hospital or giggling at a funeral. A serious hush permeated the room as Keith gave a serious account of how God had come into his life, and what Christ had meant to him each day since then.

There was something very real about the fact of death that day. As Keith spoke, I think everyone in that room was thinking of the fact that eternity is but one heartbeat—or one bite of chicken—away at any moment.

There is no place for smugness.

"We walk by faith, not by sight" (2 Corinthians 5:7).

THE LOST SANDAL

It was a cold, windy, rainy, miserable morning as I returned home from my long daily walk along the coast from Marina del Rey to Santa Monica and back.

With the rain pounding down, I was walking rapidly along when I happened to notice a child's small sandal lying on the rain-soaked walkway. I continued on in my quick pace, anxious to get out of the foul weather, but somehow I just didn't feel right. I stopped and looked back at the little sandal. It seemed so lonely out there in the rain. It didn't seem right to go on and leave it there.

I walked back, picked it up, and put it in the pocket of my rain jacket. Then I hurried on home.

There, I took the little white sandal out of my pocket and had a long look at it. As I studied it, questions flooded my mind. Had it been worn by a little boy or a little girl? Hmm? *Definitely a girl's style*, I thought.

Who is the little girl who lost this shoe? Is she blonde or brunette, or maybe a redhead? Is she thin or chubby? What is the color of her eyes? How old is she? What kind of parents does she have? Where is she now? How did she happen to lose her sandal?

I did not have an answer to any of these questions. All I could do was wonder. All I had was a child's lonely sandal left out in the cold with the rain pelting down on it. But as I stood there holding that small wet sandal and wondering about the child who lost it, I was reminded of how Jesus talked about a child when He told us how we must enter the kingdom of heaven.

Jesus says, "Truly, I say to you, unless you turn and become like children, you will never enter the kingdom of heaven" (Matthew 18:3).

The "weakness" of a child is somehow very powerful. A child demonstrates the power to wonder, the power to forgive and forget, the power to show genuine and refreshing innocence.

A child is full of trust. Jesus says that entrance into heaven demands the same spirit as that of a trusting child.

Figuratively speaking, none of us can enter the kingdom of heaven walking straight up. We will enter humbly, on our knees, or we won't enter at all. There is no place for false bravado or any sense of being adequate alone to face the harsh realities of life and death. We must each become as a little child.

The prophet once said, "A little child shall lead them" (Isaiah 11:6). Even when the little child is not there. But the reminder is there.

A little lonely sandal out in the rain.

WALKING THROUGH DARKNESS

When I was in my late teens, a neighbor, Joe Nixon, invited me and two of my friends to visit his ranch in the then wide-open mountain country near Perris, California. Enthusiastically, the three of us set out from Inglewood in a Model T Ford touring car. As we drew near to the area of the ranch, the car broke down. We tried everything we knew, but the old Ford wouldn't budge.

So we started walking toward the ranch. A friendly resident in the area told us we could reach the ranch quicker if we would leave the road and cut across the open fields. He said we were not far from the Nixon ranch, and if we would just keep to the left of the mountain in the distance, we would find the ranch close by. No problem.

It sounded so simple. We set out across the rolling, roadless terrain. It was late in the afternoon. Too late, as it turned out. As we plodded along, the terrain became rougher and our progress became slower. Then darkness fell. Very suddenly, it seemed. We could no longer see the mountain we were supposed to be aiming at. This was that real, dark, dark kind of darkness. I could barely see my hand in front of my face.

It was then that I remembered there were rattlesnakes in this country. And that they came out in the dark. After that, every crackle of every twig underfoot was a rattlesnake ready to strike. Every clump of underbrush brought visions of fangs full of venom.

I felt a growing panic. Total darkness. No lights. No moon. No stars. No trees or other objects. Just total, enveloping darkness. I was scared. We all were.

Which way do we go now? Unable to see the ground, we would stumble, bump into each other, run into sagebrush, and fall over rocks. And always, those rattlesnake fangs were potentially lurking. My heart was pounding and my hands were sweating as I groped my way along, straining to see something, anything, in that darkness that engulfed us.

Then it happened! Two small specks of light appeared in the darkness ahead. We began to have renewed hope as the two lights became larger and drew closer. Soon we heard the sound of a motor vehicle. The three of us ran and stumbled toward the lights. As we came closer, we yelled and yelled. There was no three-part harmony, just three very loud, very desperate voices.

The vehicle stopped. Between our puffing and panting, we explained our plight. The two hunters were sympathetic, and they drove us to the ranch, a short distance away, in their pick-up truck.

Being engulfed in darkness is a terrible experience. It was so that night a long time ago. It still is today. It always is.

As we walk through life, many times the darkness suddenly falls on our path. We cannot see our way. We become fearful. We panic. We stumble. We fall. We don't know which way to go. Then a light appears on the horizon. We hear the voice of Jesus saying, "I am the light of the world; he who follows me will not walk in darkness, but will have the light of life" (John 8:12).

With this promise in our hearts, we can say with Job—

"By his light I walked through darkness" (Job 29:3).

ONE STEP AT A TIME

I now love to walk.

Every morning, rain or shine, I walk one mile from my home down to the Pacific Ocean, and then, turning north, I walk three miles alongside the pounding surf, then out to the end of the historic Santa Monica Pier, the utmost point of my outward journey.

As I stand there, high above the waves, invigorated from my walk, and before heading back home, I am full of gratitude and thanksgiving to God that I am still alive to appreciate the beauty and the life I see around me. I give thanks that I am still able to experience the expansive sea, the clear blue sky, the frothy surf; still able to feel the soft white sand underfoot, the sunshine beaming down, the brisk breezes blowing off the ocean; still able to watch the dramatic transformations as the seasons come and go, as the tides ebb and flow, as storms hit and then recede.

I am especially grateful because four years ago, after triple by-pass surgery, I was unable to walk to the sidewalk in front of my house to pick up the newspaper. Now I stride along for miles, taking deep breaths of the clean salt air. It's good to be alive. Praise the Lord!

But there were some things I had to learn all over again. First, I learned that the only way to walk was to start walking. Sitting in a comfortable chair wondering and planning wouldn't do the job. Or remembering how well I used to be able to walk.

I learned that as I walked, my legs got stronger and my balance and body control improved. As I walked, my distance increased. The more I walked, the easier it was to walk. The farther I walked, the more enjoyment I got out of it. My confidence increased.

I learned not to keep looking back to see how far I had come. This brought anxiety and discouragement. *Is that all the distance I've covered?* I also learned not to try to look ahead all the way to my goal in the distance. It looked too far away, too impossible, too discouraging. I would be tempted to turn around and go home right away.

Then I made a discovery. Not a new insight, but a great one. Just take one step at a time.

I learned that by simply taking one step at a time, one step after another, the distance would take care of itself. When I did this, I found I could quit trying to mark my progress all the time and start really taking in the sights, the people, the activity, and all the interesting experiences along the way. By just putting one foot in front of the other, I found I could really enjoy the trip. And do you know what? I found I also made good progress—without thinking about making progress.

It is a lesson for life. When we keep looking back, we become discouraged with our progress. It seems we haven't really gotten anywhere for all the effort. When we strain our eyes into the future, the trip seems impossible and the destination seems out of reach. We feel we can't make it. We're tempted to quit.

God wants us to walk by faith. One day at a time. One moment at a time.

"We walk by faith, not by sight" (2 Corinthians 5:7).

Learn to walk by faith, one day at a time. Take just one step at a time.

God will take care of the distance.

POSTSCRIPT

Wistfully, this will be the final edition of *Dear You*. After numerous years, I find it necessary to terminate this weekly communication with the countless friends of the Church of the Marina. Let me hurry to assure you, I am neither fatigued nor have I lost interest in the precious subject.

You see, I am no longer with you in earthly presence but have gone on to be with my Lord in that "house not made by the hands of man—eternal in the heavens." But before a last goodbye, let me elaborate upon the unanticipated but exciting events leading to my earthly departure.

Of course, many of you were with me on Easter Sunday at the Marina Church. My heart was filled with joy in the Lord at the fine attendance. I even had the opportunity to view the video recording of my final sermon. Truly, God has blessed His work in the harbor, and we give Him all the praise.

Monday—the day after Easter—began like most other days. Following early breakfast, I ventured out on my customary walk along the beachfront in the direction of Santa Monica. I had made this walk countless times and never tired of the sea breeze and the lively greetings from the merchants along the way. My spirits were high and my heart still sang from the joy of the previous day. I was content with life. God had been good and life seemed worthwhile.

On the return journey to the church office, however, something grand and glorious occurred. My aging heart gave way and, in a matter of moments, I strode boldly out into the breath-taking presence of my Maker. The transition from a much-faulted life here on earth to life eternal was swift and void of pain.

There was no time for last minute recollections or reflections. Had there been, my thoughts would have been with my precious family and the church family at the Marina. Now securely wrapped within the folds of the Master's robe and far from the trials of life on earth, I pray the work of the Church of the Marina will continue under the leadership of yet another shepherd.

Until we meet again at the Savior's feet—goodbye and God bless. Keep the faith. "I am with you always, to the close of the age" (Matthew 28:20).

PASTOR DON ROBERTSON
(written by his brother, Doug)